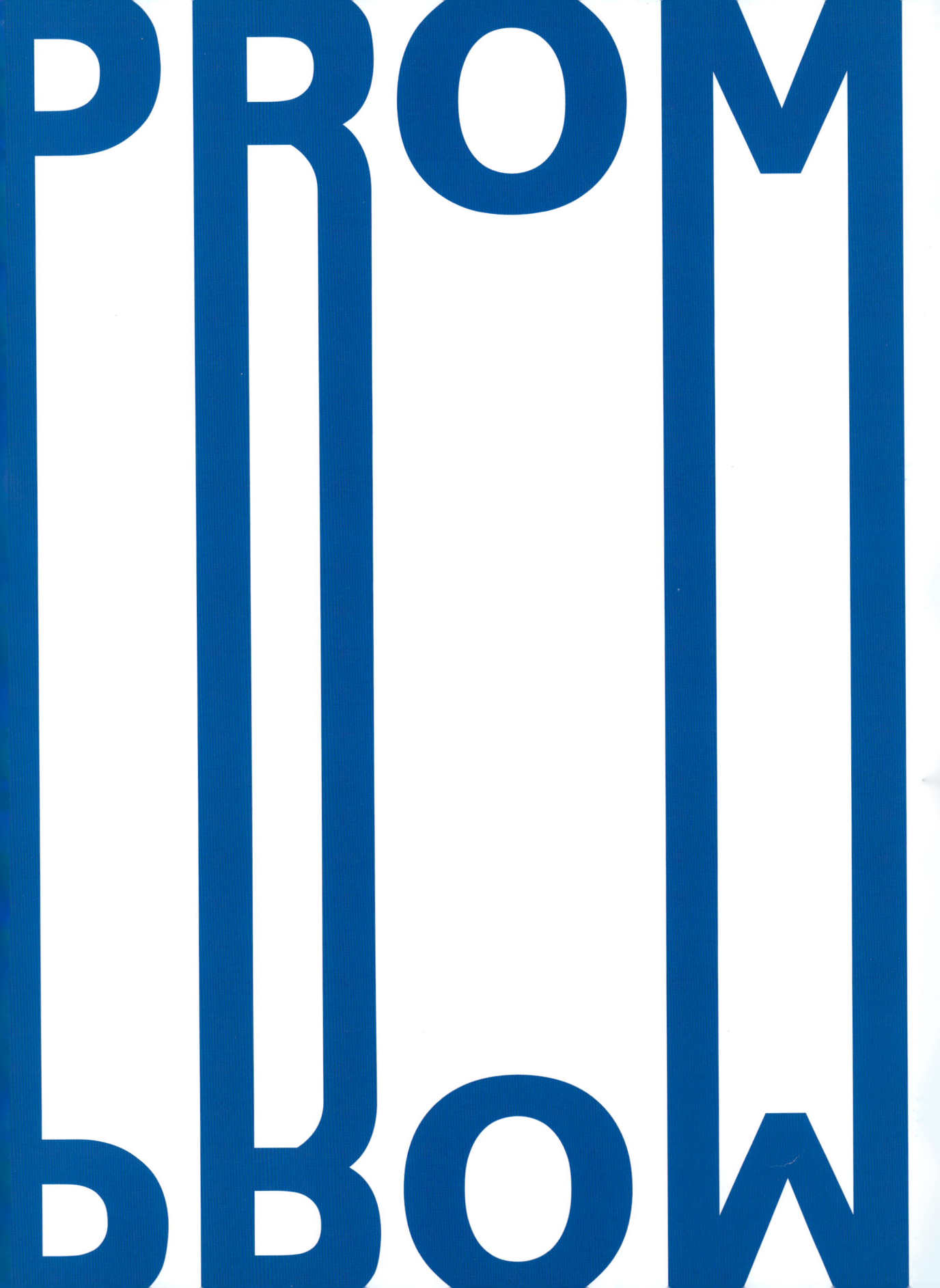

Bottom

PROMOTION

bottom

PROMOTION

©2013 CHOIS PUBLISHING INC.

All rights reserved. No part of this publication may be reproduced, stored in retrieval system or transmitted in any form or by any means without the publisher's written permission. The copyright on the individual texts and design works is held by the respective designers and contributors.

ISBN 978-1-61175-034-8 / 1-61175-034-2

CHOIS PUBLISHING INC.
P.O.Box 4389, Road Town, Tortola, British Virgin Islands
China Office
Unit 1201, Anji Plaza, 760 S. Xizang Rd.,
Shanghai 200011, China
Email: info@choisgallery.com
Phone: +86 21 6346 0711/10

Publisher
David Choi

Editorial & Art Department
Editorial Director _ Lynn Lin
Senior Editor _ Cynthia Hsu
cynthia@choisgallery.com
Proofreading Editor _ Susie Gordon
Designer _ Haiou Hu

Marketing & Sales Department
Advertising Inquiries _ Claudia Chen
claudia.chen@choisgallery.com

Sales Executive (Overseas) _ Shannon Ye
dist@choisgallery.com

Subscriptions _ Pete Yu
pete@choisgallery.com

Marketing Manager (China) _ Nomi Wu
wuguo@choisgallery.com

Distributor
Chois Publishing Inc. Taiwan office
No. 11, Section 3, Hépíng East Rd, Daan District, Taipei City 10675, Taiwan
Phone: 02-23042764

Kili China
Unit 1201, Anji Plaza, 760 S. Xizang Rd.,
Shanghai 200011, China
Phone: +86 21 6346 0711/10
info@choisgallery.com

Share Your Genius With The Global Peers.
Please visit www.choisgallery.com or contact Cynthia Hsu:
cynthia@choisgallery.com to contribute your fantastic work.
Printed and Bound in China

SHARING THE WISDOM OF GLOBAL INNOVATION

PREFACE

In a scientific sense, the art world contains no initiators or precursors. However, unlike science, the works of our predecessors do not constitute an acquired truth from which anyone who follows after can profit. That is why today, even if you try your best to write, it is not possible to match great writers like Homer.

Most of us are just passengers in the creative field, but we thirst for our peers' experiences in creating. In the meantime, we like to share our accomplishments with them. It is hard to believe that in this era of free information, what we know is still limited and incomplete. The Internet, which most people believe to be a panacea, brings too much confusion and too many choices, and this truth is unfortunately neglected.

In the past two years, Chois Publishing Inc has published a series of magazines and books about the creative industry, such as Gallery (the world's best graphics) bimonthly, Workshop bimonthly and Choi's Package quarterly. We prefer print media—the traditional way to spread new ideas—because we believe that it holds inherent value and is a better way to showcase the work in detail. More importantly, it displays the integrity and ability required in this "hand-made" industry.

To quote George Bernard Shaw: "If you have an apple and I have an apple and we exchange apples, then you and I will still each have one apple. But if you have an idea and I have an idea and we exchange these ideas, then each of us will have two ideas."

Through this "SHARING PLAN" we hope to facilitate the exchange of ideas. We are not merely focusing on the graphics, but dealing with the whole creative industry, including architecture, interiors, fashion, and product design. We warmly welcome you to join us.

With thanks.

The Editor

12-99
CAMPAIGN

- 14 GOLF GTI BAG
- 15 HEINEKEN PUB RUGBY
- 16 HANG HOLZINGER
- 18 NOT YOUR EVERYDAY EVERYDAY
- 20 TODO PARA CHEBAR SS11
- 22 INTERNATIONAL FILM FESTIVAL ROTTERDAM XL
- 24 THE ESCAPIST FANTASY TOURISM BOARD
- 26 PURPLE
- 28 TAG HEUER
- 30 GREEN DESIGN FESTIVAL
- 32 TALES OF COLT 45
- 36 UNITED COUNTRIES OF BASEBALL
- 40 DUCK AND COVER: ADVERTISING CAMPAIGN, GARMENT GRAPHICS & COLLATERA
- 44 POINT TO POINT
- 45 WORLD'S LARGEST PEN DRIVE
- 46 AISHTI CAMPAIGN
- 52 LEAVE YOUR MARK
- 54 AIZONE 11
- 56 AIZONE FW12
- 58 SHORT STORIES
- 60 STAIN BROIDERY – TIDE DETERGENTS
- 61 BOYSEN FLOWERS SERIES
- 62 THE SYDNEY INTERNATIONAL FOOD FESTIVAL
- 64 ADIDAS "FAMOUS IN AFRICA" CAMPAIGN
- 66 DRINKS
- 67 OUTRAGEOUS
- 68 WAY OF INFINITI – M LAUNCH CAMPAIGN
- 70 NEW YEARS POSTER
- 71 PERRIER JOUËT CHAMPAGNE AD CAMPAIGN
- 72 TOYOTA
- 74 JOB BAGS
- 76 BILLY BLUE SCHOOL OF DESIGN
- 77 CLEARASIL DREAMS
- 78 ATOMIK FALL WINTER CAMPAIGN 2011
- 80 TURKISH AIRLINES: NETWORK MAPS
- 84 128 STARS – 1 ORCHESTRA
- 88 KNIGHTS TOURNAMENT
- 89 ROMAN RETURN TICKET
- 90 UTRECHT CITY THEATRE'S NEW CULTURAL SEASON
- 92 EVERGREEN
- 93 IKEA HOLIDAY CAMPAIGN
- 94 ZIMBABWEAN
- 96 ARTABAC 2011
- 98 ULURUFF

100-145
CATALOGUE BROCHURE LEAFLET

- 102 WORLDLY CARES AND LOVE AFFAIRS
- 103 CALLE BRAND NEWSPRINT
- 104 ZPYZ
- 106 ILOVEDUST BLACK BOOK
- 108 BUNCH OF STARS
- 110 VERBO 2010
- 111 ENJOY YOUR KITCHEN
- 112 10TH ANNIVERSARY IDENTITY FOR DEPARTMENT OF ARCHITECTURE
- 114 DH14
- 116 COLOMBIAGE
- 118 MICHELL YARN PROMO BROCHURE
- 119 RESTAURANT HINDENBURG
- 120 ESTORIL FASHION ART FESTIVAL
- 124 CHECK POINT
- 125 PAUL WEEKS PROMO
- 126 MAK
- 130 TWENTY FOUR
- 131 ST KILDA FESTIVAL 2011
- 132 CHANGING PERSPECTIVES | CHANGING FUTURES
- 134 TARGET MICHAEL GRAVES
- 136 TEL
- 138 CONTEMPORARY SLOVENIAN HUMANISTS & SOCIAL SCIENTISTS
- 140 WAKE FOREST UNIVERSITY FOOTBALL
- 142 WALL & DECÒ
- 144 TORREMAT CATALOGUE

CONTENT

146-171 DIRECT MAIL

- 148 A BIGGER HARVEST
- 149 AMENA DISCOTHEQUE
- 150 AN ORANGE THAT TOOK ON A NEW LIFE
- 152 THE BEER THAT CAME AT THE RIGHT TIME
- 154 ORIGAMI INVITATION
- 156 ERSTE BANK
- 158 BIGGER IS POSSIBLE
- 159 FAST AND EASY
- 160 HARLEY-DAVIDSON HANDLEBARS 2011 CALENDAR
- 161 COMFORT PILLOW
- 162 IKEA FLAT PACK DIRECT MAILER
- 164 A FAT MAILING FOR DERMASOLUTIONS
- 165 EQUIPADOS
- 166 STOP THE NODDING
- 168 JAMES NEWMAN
- 170 A PICTURE SPEAKS A THOUSAND WORDS

172-189 NAME CARD

- 174 ANIMAL X-RAY BUSINESS CARDS
- 175 CAROLINE BOISVERT
- 176 PAT & CO, BRAND COACH
- 177 TOY CAR
- 178 EBOLAINDUSTRIES' IDENTITY
- 179 ÁNGELES RUBIO
- 180 CORA HILLEBRAND IDENTITY
- 182 CONTACT 2.0
- 184 FINANCIAL ADVISOR BUSINESS CARD
- 185 NORBURN MODEL AIRCRAFT SUPPLY BUSINESS CARD
- 186 ARIS NASIOS BUSINESS CARD
- 187 STRANGE DESIGN NAMECARD
- 188 UNDERSIZED RECESSION BUSINESS CARDS

190-203 PACKAGE

- 192 DOSS BLOCKOS BEER
- 193 BUILD YOUR OWN
- 194 TANQ
- 196 EYEPET
- 197 RE-PACK
- 198 JIMMY'S ICED COFFEE
- 200 VERY VERY BRIGHT
- 201 OH MY DOG!
- 202 RETHINK TABLE WINE

204-235 PROMOTION GIFT AND GOODS

- 206 SOLLI DISKOKLUBB / TREKKFUGL
- 208 BFG MIMOBOT FLASH DRIVES
- 209 PLANT
- 210 EIZO Pin-up Calendar
- 212 HOLIDAY LOG
- 213 SAMPLING TOOL
- 214 ONE DAILY DROP
- 215 PERSONAL TRAINER
- 216 HAND DESIGN STUDIO DEVILISH FOOD GIFT BOX
- 217 KERSCHOFFSET PROMOTIONAL GIFT — NUANCES MAKE THE DIFFERENCE
- 218 PANTOGAR MEMO PAD
- 219 BUILD YOUR YEAR OF GOOD DEEDS
- 220 LET'S PLAY WITH FOOD
- 221 ARJOWIGGINS CURIOUS PARTICLES NOTEBOOK
- 222 MATTER STRATEGIC DESIGN 2011 NOTEBOOK
- 223 DIFFUSEUR DE BONHEUR
- 224 SEASON'S GREETINGS 2010/2011
- 225 TWOTHOUSAND11
- 226 YESTERDAY WAS A BORE
- 227 SAYHELLO ON YOUR DESK
- 228 AKTION MENSCH ANNUAL REPORT 2011
- 230 JACK AND THE GIANT RECESSION SELF-PROMOTIONAL BOOK 2011
- 231 WINTER WEDDING INVITATION
- 232 THE ALLOTMENT SELF-PROMOTIONAL MATERIALS
- 234 COPIER CALENDAR

BOTTOM

CAMPAIGN 1

Client _
Volkswagen
Agency _
.V.
Creative Director _
Christian Vince
Art Director _
Guillaume Meriaux
Copywriter _
Adrien Plouard
Country _
France

GOLF GTI BAG

Every Mondial de l'Automobile — the world's biggest motorshow — Volkswagen offers bags to the visitors in order to drive as much traffic towards Volkswagen's booth as possible (competition is fierce at motorshows).
This year, we decided to make a bag a bit different, a bit more eye-catching.
So, we designed this trompe-l'oeil bag, as a tribute to the mythical Golf GTI and its drivers' tendency known to brag.
This was such a success that most of the visitors kept the bag after the tradeshow, bringing even more visibility to the brand. That's why Volkswagen decided to distribute the bag to clients in the brand showrooms too.

HEINEKEN PUB RUGBY

Heineken is the official sponsor of the Dubai Rugby Sevens. The premium tasting Lager wanted to engage rugby fans and beer drinkers before the tournament. Ordinary tent cards and coasters weren't going to cut it, so we decided to cut them.
We turned standard promotional material into a captivating bar game. Within only two days of launching our new game in key outlets, we received countless mentions via Facebook and Twitter as well as popular blogs in this region.
Weeks leading up to the game day, delighted beer drinkers were challenging their mates to a game of Pub Rugby whilst enjoying an ice cold Heineken.

Client _
Heineken
Agency _
Memac Ogilvy
Creative Director _
Ramzi Moutran
Art Director _
Leo Rosa Borges, Gary Rolf
Copywriter _
Ali Mokdad
Designers _
Leo Rosa Borges, Tamzin Hoets
Country _
United Arab Emirates

Client _
Chris Holzinger
Studio _
Eps51 Graphic Design Studio
Country _
Germany

HANG HOLZINGER

The outdoor advertisement for Chris Holzinger's showroom and collection SS 2010 Berlin was based on the idea put forward by fashion designer Chris Holzinger to promote his showroom at Berlin Fashion Week 2009 where he exhibited his Spring/Summer 2010 collection: "Attract people's attention — stay within a reasonable budget."
We simply handprinted the title, place and date onto his old specimen and hung them 5–7 metres high all over Berlin Mitte. For this reason, we developed a stencil version of Bodoni Bold Italic.

Client _
Monoprix
Agency _
Havas City
Creative Director _
Florence Bellisson
Art Director _
Jean Michel Alirol
Copywriter _
Dominique Marchand
Designers _
Cleo Charuet, Deroudilhe Arnaud
3D Illustrator _
Baptiste Masse
Country _
France

NOT YOUR EVERYDAY EVERYDAY

CHALLENGE: Daily life should never be routine
Monoprix is France's leading city centre supermarket chain for all the needs of daily life.
With the recession, a sense of gloom has pervaded people's day-to-day lives. Our answer to this was OPTIMISM — a rejection of the ordinary and an injection of magic into the everyday. Our message was that Daily Life should never be routine.

IDEA: Let the product be the ad campaign!
Our idea was to create a sensation using the product itself as the advertising medium.
2000 different packagings were created to give more visibility and a refreshing, eye-catching impact to Monoprix's daily products. Paying tribute to Pop Art and readopting the bayadere style of the brand's communication, we chose a colour and militant look which is both straight and cheerful. The products are not shown, but exclusively named on their packagings in big capital letters, creating a clear and graphic design.
Each product has a unique, amusing phrase or witty word play.
The design highlights Monoprix's message: daily life should be beautiful and funny.

RESULTS
The campaign was a huge success with articles in the press, on the web, and hundreds of reactions on social networks.
+ 20% increase in sales of tinned tomatoes
+ 0,1 increase in market share
+ 1,5 increase in Monoprix's popularity index
In 2010 Monoprix surpassed previous income records with a 4-billion net profit.

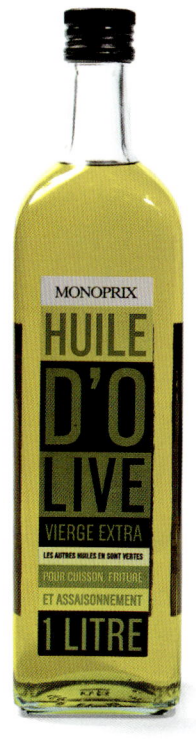

Client _
Jazmin Chebar
Agency _
POGO
Creative Director _
Pampa Garcia Peña
Art Director _
Ardi Carlos Grygierczyk
Photographer _
**Pampa Garcia Peña,
Ardi Carlos Grygierczyk,
Micaela Bueno**
Country _
Argentina

TODO PARA CHEBAR SS11

Todo para Chebar is Jazmin Chebar's sales claim. They use vintage photos of women in different situations, in this case we came up with the idea of using a photo of Beatles fans gretting a plane with the euphoric characteristic of the time. We added lots of Jazmin's shopping bags in the photo and real ones in the window display, so the photo interact with the shopping bags in the window display. Continuing with this idea, we also made some min-bags that came with real shopping bags. This project was carried out in collaboration with the Jazmin Chebar's image team.

CAMPAIGN

Client _
International Film Festival Rotterdam (IFFR)
Studio _
75B
Country _
The Netherlands

INTERNATIONAL FILM FESTIVAL ROTTERDAM XL

In 2009 we designed the new identity for the International Film Festival Rotterdam.
The logo comprises a tiger's head and the name of the festival in capitals, both elements in black & white. The image is based on quick do-it-yourself drawing of symbols from subcultures like the anarchy/peace symbol.
This design underlines the idiosyncratic and future-oriented character of the IFFR. The tiger makes eye contact, stares straight at you and evokes a reaction — just like the festival, which wants to provoke with its program.
(Social interaction is an important theme of the festival. In the design, we want people to participate with this interaction.)
This design is the base for the XL campaign poster.
Because the festival has existed for 40 years, they made the program XL. Also 40 written-in Roman numerals is "XL". On top of the basic black and white IFFR identity we drew XL as big as possible on all different formats, with different colour markers, in contrast with the elemental black/white tiger.

Client _
The Escapist Fantasy Tourism Board
Designer/Illustrator _
Alex Egner
Country _
USA

THE ESCAPIST FANTASY TOURISM BOARD

This campaign, which promotes dissociative mental leisure excursions, was created as a satirical advertising campaign for The Escapist Fantasy Tourism Board. The components include a tourism brochure and a series of 6 individual posters which combine to create a continuous landscape, spelling out the word ESCAPE.

CAMPAIGN

PURPLE

This work was created for McCann Oslo and was part of the launch of Netcom's new identity campaign. Together with photographer Pål Laukli, a set of strange purple images was made to introduce the colour purple as the new identity colour for Netcom.

Client _
McCann / Netcom
Studio _
Anti
Creative Director _
Tore Woll/McCann, Kjetil Wold/Anti
Copywriter _
Erlend Klouman
Designers _
Fredrik Melby, Martin Yang Stousland
Photographer _
Pål Laukli
Country _
Norway

Client _
Tag Heuer
Studio _
ANTI
Creative Director _
Fabien Moullard/Bbdo
Art Director _
Mark Forgan
Copywriter _
Jamie Standen
Designers _
Endre Berentzen, Robert Dalen
3D _
Baptiste Masse
Country _
Norway

TAG HEUER

Retouch job for Tag Heuer to showcase the mastery of accuracy.

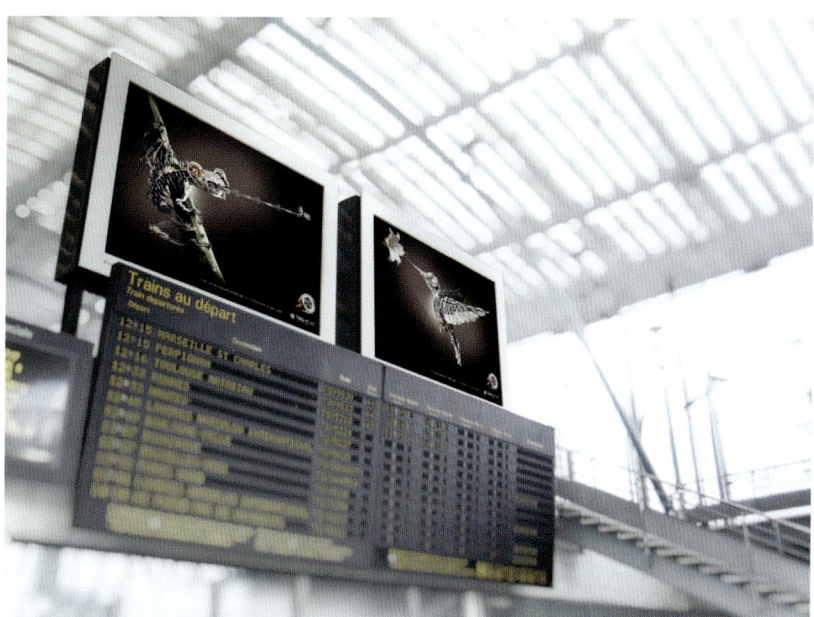

Client _
Brainlab
Agency _
Busybuilding
Creative Director _
Dimitris Gkazis
Art Director _
Dimitris Gkazis
Copywriter _
Nikos Palaiologos
Designers _
Dimitris Gkazis, Kostis Sotirakos, Vicky Nitsopoulou
Country _
Greece

GREEN DESIGN FESTIVAL

Design of the campaign and signage of Green Design Festival, a biennial open-air, open-to all project which examines the repercussions of climate change through the prism provided by the various fields of design.

Client _
Pabst / Colt 45
Agency _
Cole & Weber United
Creative Director _
Todd Grant
Art Director _
Scott Fero, Jim Mahfood
Copywriter _
Jacob Baas, Jim Mahfood
Designers _
Scott Fero, Jim Mahfood, Dave McKeague
Illustrator _
Jim Mahfood
Country _
USA

TALES OF COLT 45

The Tales of Colt 45 was an interactive world of street-art-style graphic novels, and it provided involving content people sought after and encouraged them to share their stories to help shape the campaign.

We partnered with cult graphic novelist Jim Mahfood to create an integrated campaign that included a full-blown graphic novel, wild postings, outdoor, print, a participatory website with multiple webisodes, unique POS and wall murals. Each execution was illustrated in black and white on a brown bag background to capture the true simplicity and appreciation for the brown paper bag so well known to the Malt beverage category, in particular Colt 45.

We involved our target by partnering with *Vice Magazine* to create a cross-country party tour and gather people's stories to be published in a series of limited edition fanzines. →

The tales and their creators came out of the woodwork. Colt's 16oz. bottle experienced double-digit sales growth – driven by a younger male drinker. The website is a great expression and interaction point for the revived brand. Within a few months, we surpassed traffic expectations by double digit percentages and engaged hundreds of thousands of new ambassadors – each spending 2 ½ minutes+/visit. People have blogged about the campaign and posted their own tales across Flickr, YouTube and other networks. And, the level of interest in our *Vice Magazine* fanzines has made it a staple content source for the publication. ←

Client _
Nike / Major League Baseball
Agency _
Cole & Weber United
Creative Director _
Todd Grant
Art Director _
Todd Derksen
Copywriter _
Mike Tuton
Designer _
Todd Derksen
Illustrator _
David Reinbold
Country _
USA

UNITED COUNTRIES OF BASEBALL

United Countries of Baseball (UCOB) was designed to help Nike & Major League Baseball brand their retail partnership in a way that celebrated the fan experience.

The idea engaged the most hardcore fans of each MLB team by mapping the geographic boundaries of fan loyalty while providing encyclopaedic information of each land mass as if they were actual countries and exploring each team's myths, legends, rivalries and "exports and imports".

Started as in-stadium posters, the idea expanded to apparel, outdoor, online, rival, live action, and a proprietary voting application that allowed citizens to "take over" the map drawing for future seasons.

Our fully integrated approach brought retail and fan environments together and encouraged fans to add power to the idea.

UCOB debuted in stadium team stores across all 30 markets, with additional print support in selected markets. And knowing Niketown would be a popular stop for All Star Game attendees, we created a fully branded experience around the area. The program included exterior wraps, rooftop billboards, floor-to-ceiling banners, voting drives, in-store swearing-in ceremonies for new "fan citizens", and a new line of United Countries of Baseball apparel.

Each channel fueled activism by asking each fan to pledge their allegiance.

We initiated a wide reaching conversation between fans both online and off. One citizen of the game got the Internet buzzing when the United Countries of Baseball map appeared on Flickr.com. From Dead Spin and Barstool Sports to Strangemaps.com to the Gawker network, over 60,000 blogs were talking, or rather, fervently debating the map.

And so for the playoffs, a unique voting application allowed over 30,000 fans to vote by zip code and purchase newly created season-to-season apparel.

Every online retail outlet (niketown.com, mlb.com, amazon.com and bodog.com) sold out of the apparel and the maps in two weeks.

 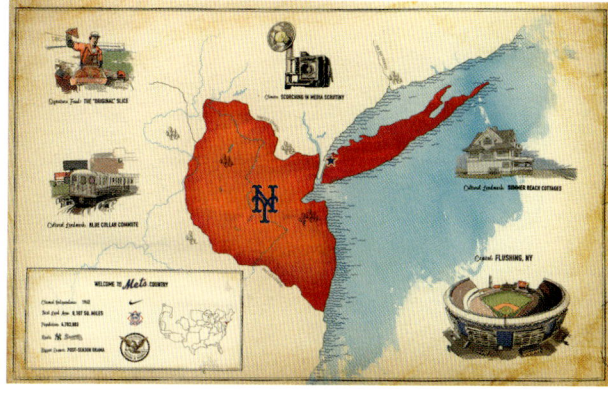

CAMPAIGN | 37

Client _
Duck and Cover
Studio _
Design Friendship
Designers _
Natasha Shah, Chris Hilton
Country _
UK

DUCK AND COVER: ADVERTISING CAMPAIGN, GARMENT GRAPHICS & COLLATERAL

Initially briefed to collaborate with the brand's design team to create seasonal garment graphics, our input was quickly sought across the brand's other creative and marketing collateral.

Over the last four seasons we have creatively lead the garment graphics, packaging, brand positioning and the ATL advertising campaigns.

The brand inspiration is based upon utilitarian, industrial and military themes that not only influence the marketing and in-store campaigns, but also affects the approach to garment detailing, fabrics and cut.

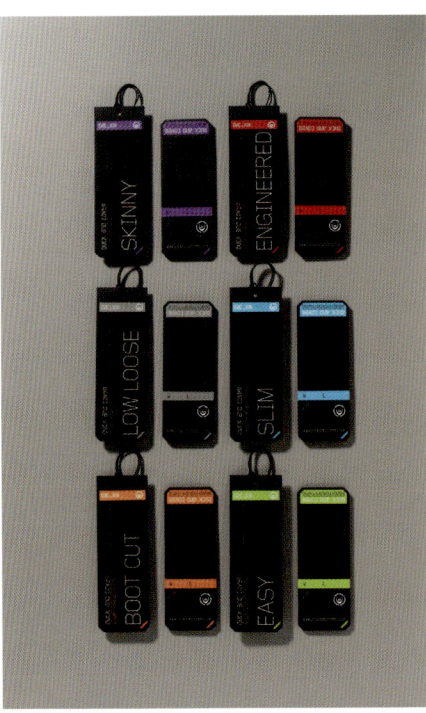

WWW.DUCKANDCOVER.CO.UK

Client _
Hong Kong Youth Arts Foundation
Studio _
Gardens & Co.
Creative Director _
Wilson Tang
Art Director _
Wilson Tang
Designers _
Jeffrey Tam, Wong Kin Chung
Region _
Hong Kong

POINT TO POINT

Initiated by Hong Kong Youth Arts Foundation, 1,500 young participants have created innovative site-specific art installations and dance performances for 8 locations – Embark on a journey, REDISCOVER Hong Kong. This year is the second year. We redefined the event identity and the visual system.

WORLD'S LARGEST PEN DRIVE

Kingston Technology, the world's largest independent manufacturer of memory products, wanted to highlight the fact that though pen drives look small, they are huge storage devices. They wanted to drive home the magnitude of space of Kingston pen drives to customers.

Also, Kingston's main USP is storage and space. It boasts of having the largest pen drive. Hence, the task for the creative team was to figure out a way by which the message "a lot can be stored in just one pen drive" could get conveyed.

The idea was to create an illusion of a huge pen drive and have people walking into it. Team Six Inches created the installation of an actual pen drive, with the dimension of: 31ft×9.5ft×2ft. This installation, therefore, successfully showcased the experience of space.

Nirmal Lifestyle, one of the largest shopping malls in Mumbai, was chosen for the installation since this is a place that attracts a large number of footfalls, especially on weekends.

Client _
Kingston Technology
Agency _
Six Inches Communication Pvt. Ltd.
Chief Creative _
Pravin Shah
ACD - Art _
Reshma Basankar
ACD - Copy _
Amit Badle
Art Director _
Rutul Mistry
Country _
India

Creative Director _
Stefan Sagmeister
Art Direction & Design _
Jessica Walsh
Photographer _
Bela Borsodi (FW11)
Henry Haargreaves (FW12)
3D art _
3D Agency
Model Making _
Prop Art
Country _
USA

AISHTI CAMPAIGN

Design & direction for the Fall/Winter advertising campaign of Aishti, a luxury department store in the Middle East. Images were printed in newspapers, magazines, and billboards throughout Lebanon.

CAMPAIGN | 47

CAMPAIGN 2

Client _
Sharpie
Studio _
Hom+Gang
Creative Director _
Lauren Hom, Jessie Gang
Copywriter _
Lauren Hom
Designer _
Jessie Gang
Country _
Hong Kong

LEAVE YOUR MARK

This print campaign for Sharpie demonstrates the permanence of the product by utilising historical figures that left long-lasting marks on society.

CAMPAIGN

Creative Direction _
Stefan Sagmeister
Direction & Design _
Jessica Walsh
Photography _
Henry Hargreaves
Body Painting _
Anastasia Durasova
Body Painting Assistants _
Edvina Sarukhanyan, Veronika Ossi
Hair Stylist _
Gregory Alan
Retouching _
Lutz & Schmitt
Country _
USA

AIZONE 11

Art Direction & design for the Spring/Summer advertising campaign for Aizone, a luxury department store in the Middle East. Models were body painted in black and white patterns to match the signature patterns for the store. Images were printed in newspapers, magazines, and billboards throughout Lebanon.

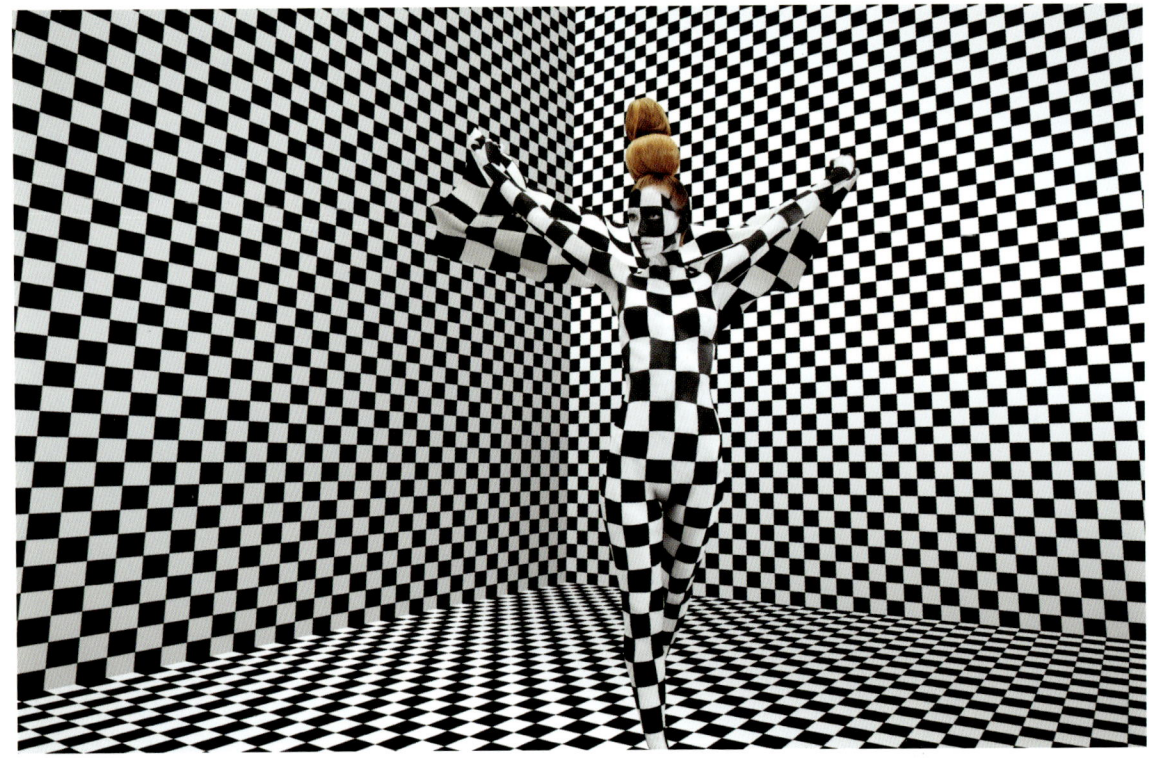

Creative Direction _
Stefan Sagmeister
Direction & Art Design _
Jessica Walsh
Photography _
Henry Hargreaves
Body Painting _
Anastasia Durasova
Hair Stylist _
Gregory Alan
Retouching _
Lutz & Schmitt
Country _
USA

AIZONE FW12

Art direction & design for the Spring/Summer advertising campaign for Aizone, a luxury department store in the Middle East. Models were body painted in typographic sentences "Forget Regret" "The Time is Now" and "Talk Less Say More". This design has been printed in newspapers, magazines, and billboards throughout Lebanon.

Client _
Hotel Emiliano
Agency _
JWT Brasil
Creative Director _
Mario D'Andrea, Roberto Fernandez
Art Director _
Sthefan Ko
Copywriters _
Luiz Filipin, Guilherme Nesti
Illustrator _
Eduardo Recife
Photographer _
Tuca Reines
Country _
Brazil

SHORT STORIES

As the precursor of small luxury hotels in Sao Paulo, Emiliano is a 5-star hotel in the city. It gained its reputation for the quality of the services, which guests did not take for granted and that yielded good stories about the hotel. The campaign explores these episodes, describing the wishes of guests that were fulfilled thanks to the efforts of the hotel staff.

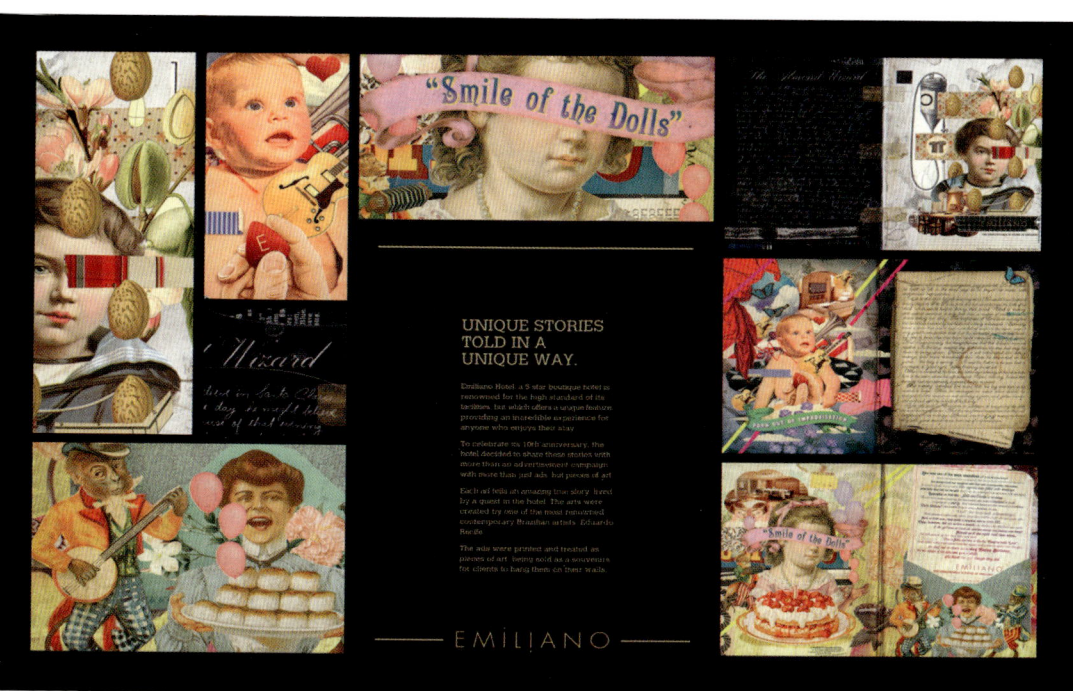

Client _
Procter & Gamble
Studio _
Leo Burnett India Mumbai, INDIA
National Creative Director _
Sridhar Leo Burnett India
Executive Creative Director _
Kb Vinod
Art Directors _
Deepak Singh, Nishant Jethi
Copywriter _
Kb Vinod
Illustrator _
Nishant Jethi
Country _
India

STAIN BROIDERY – TIDE DETERGENTS

The brief was to design an innovative & involving way to give away free sachets of Tide while staying true to brand promise, in a marketplace where it is difficult to stand out in a free sampling exercise. Cloth Posters with embroidery of a stain mark were designed. Pulling at the suspended Tide takeaway pack unravels the embroidery leaving 'stain-free' cloth behind. The sampling target was exceeded by 127%. As a bonus, the exercise also became a much talked-about advertising project for the brand.

BOYSEN FLOWERS SERIES

Boysen is the only paint company in the Philippines to be awarded with Responsible Care®, the chemical industries' global initiative for environmental safety. The achievement is a significant contribution to the company vision to be the greenest in South East Asia. Posters were created to celebrate this achievement. Using high speed photography, the team employed strobe lights, water pumps, splashing techniques, a shower head, mixing bowls and Boysen Paints to create delicate and dramatic forms of exotic flora. This effort created greater awareness for Boysen's commitment to environmental safety and helped strengthen its reputation as the number one paint manufacturer in the country.

Client _
Pacific Paint (Boysen) Philippines Inc.
Studio _
TBWA \ Santiago Mangada Puno, Makati City
Executive Creative Director _
Melvin Mangada
Creative Director _
Manuel Villafania
Copywriter _
Bryan Siy
Art Director _
Manuel Villafania, Melvin Mangada, Denise Tee
Photographer _
G-nie Arambulo
Country _
Philippines

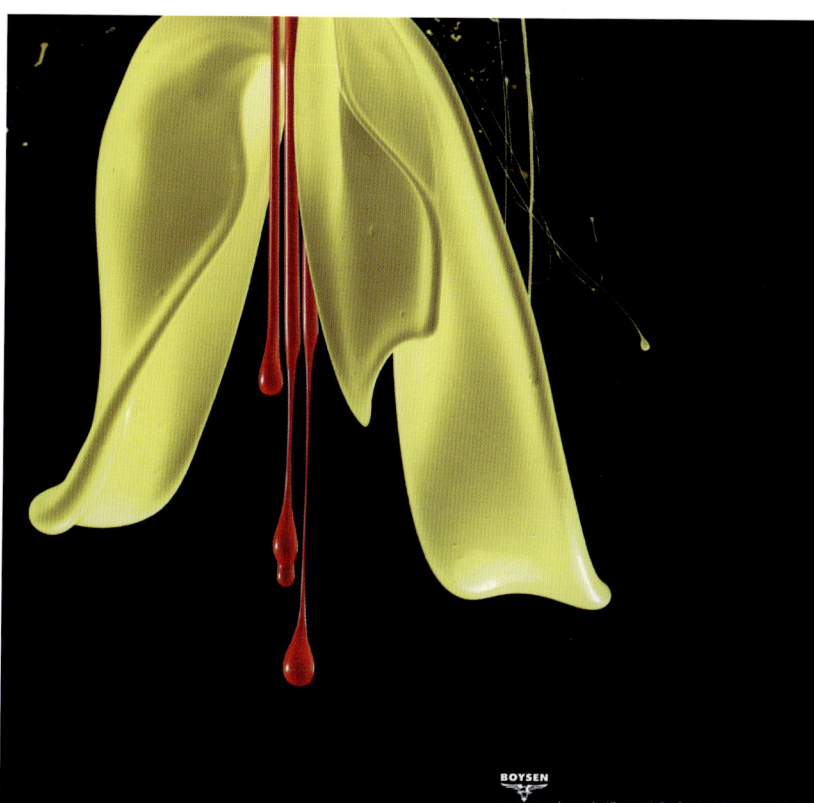

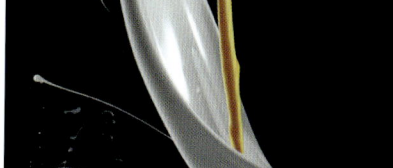
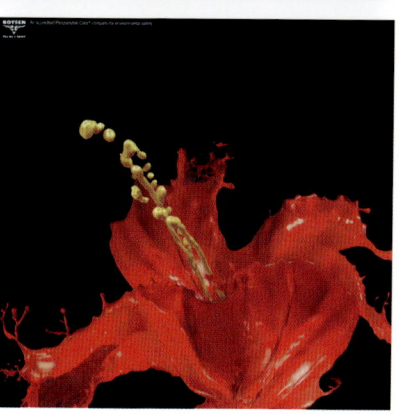

Client _
Fairfax – The Sydney Morning Herald
Studio _
Whybin/TBWA
Executive Creative Director _
Garry Horner
Creative Director _
Matt Kemsley
Art Director _
Miles Jeffreys
Copywriter _
Tammy Keegana
Agency Producer _
Sean Ascroft, Jessie Williams
Retoucher _
Nick Mueller
Account Director _
Alicia Diaz
Country _
Australia

THE SYDNEY INTERNATIONAL FOOD FESTIVAL

This year the Sydney International Food Festival replaces the popular Good Food Month, events ranging from restaurant dinners to markets, street festivals and open-air eating, the best regional product and the finest fine dining. A major highlight is the World Chef Showcase Weekend, bringing together Sydney's biggest culinary stars, as well as chefs from some of the top restaurants in the world.

The beauty of the creative idea is in its simplicity, a better way to launch an international food festival than visually unite food with one of the most common international symbols: flags. The flexibility of the concept and imagery has allowed the 'food flags' to be used across a broad range of event collateral from the event program right through to a 30sec TVC.

The campaign will span across TV, press, radio and online. It will continue to run until late October when the festival wraps up.

Client _
Adidas
Studio _
TBWA Hunt Lascaris/TBWA 180
Art Director _
Nadja Lossgott, Marion Bryan
Typographer _
Nadja Lossgott
Illustrators _
Tracey Milne, Nadja Lossgott, Sbusiso Mkhwanazi
Photographer _
David Prior, Rob Frew
Copywriter _
Nicholas Hulley
Creative Directors _
Damon Stapleton
Executive Creative Director _
John Hunt
Country _
South Africa

ADIDAS "FAMOUS IN AFRICA" CAMPAIGN

On the streets of Africa, from Cape Town to Kinshasa, from Lagos to Mombasa, the true measure of fame is having a haircut named after you on a barbershop sign. The streets are full of "The Obama", "The Oprah" and the "Snoop Dogg". This ubiquitous barbershop signage is an African graphic art form with its naïve renderings and pragmatic use of wood, metal and any material found on the streets.

To celebrate the Confederation's Cup being played for the first time on African soil, Adidas commissioned a series of "barbershop" artworks that honour their galaxy of stars like Gerrard, Messi, Kaka and Pienaar. A "cut" was created for each player according to their skill — those who deserve a haircut named after them. Every poster, print advert, in-store element and billboard was hand painted, from the type to the illustrations.

Kopanya means "together" (it is also the name of the official Confed Cup ball), which makes this campaign unique in being an African interpretation of Adidas' global positioning of 'Together I Am Strong', essentially an international brand has created an African campaign which it has sent out to the world. And it seems the soccer world has fallen in love with it, judging by the hundreds and hundreds of global websites it has appeared on.

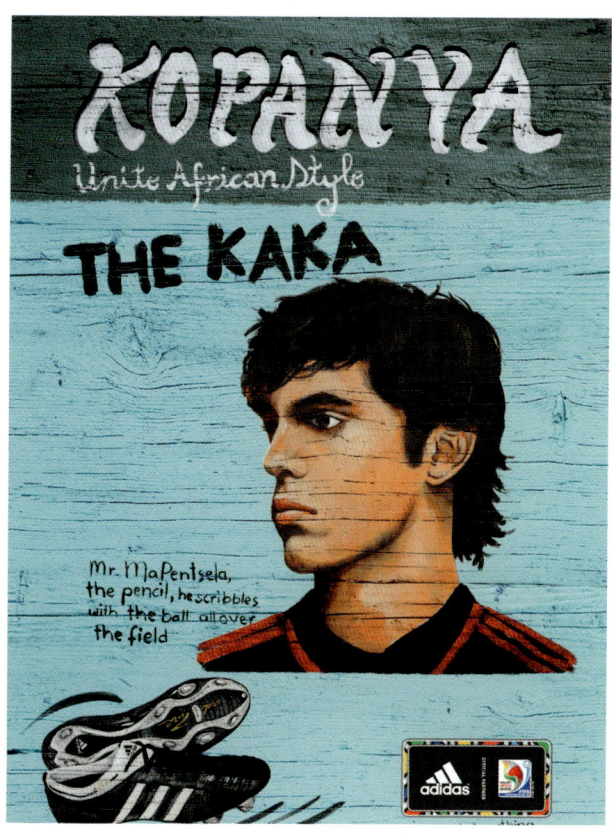

CAMPAIGN | 65

Client _
ABSOLUT VODKA
Studio _
TBWA/Chiat/Day NY
Creative Director _
Mark Figliulo
Art Director _
Jin Park
Associate Art Director _
Nicolas Troop
Photographers _
**Ellen Von Unwerth,
Amanda De Cadenet**
Country _
USA

DRINKS

As an evolution of its ongoing "DRINKS" campaign, ABSOLUT VODKA has used the bustling streets of Chicago to bring to life the unique universes created by visionary photographers, Ellen Von Unwerth and Amanda De Cadenet. With a series of bus shelter installations, ABSOLUT has leveraged the imagery of talent such as Kate Beckinsale, Zooey Deschanel & Ali Larter to transform these shelters into tactile installations for people to enjoy. Bringing to life the worlds that embody ABSOLUT "Lemon Drop", "Twist" and "Bloody", the shelters (which will run until late December) use original seating, stunning colour and even tropical plant-life.

OUTRAGEOUS

David La Chapelle chose to shoot on a beach in order to emphasis the sense of coming from the darkness into the light. From there, every element that is coming out of the iconic ABSOLUT bottle-shaped closet contributes to that sense outrageousness and freedom. All the people are representative of the LGBT community and contribute emotionally to the sense of joy and celebration of the 30 year anniversary of ABSOLUT's involvement with the community. Each element does not neccesarily "mean" something or "symbolize" something — each contributes to the whole. And each is very uniquely David — outrageous.

Client _
ABSOLUT VODKA
Agency _
TBWA Worldwide
Chairman/Chief Creative Officer _
Mark Figliulo
Creative Director _
Sue Anderson
Creative Director/Art Director _
Hoj Jomehri
Art Director _
Brantley Barefoot
Copywriter _
Jim Therkalsen
Head of Production _
Robert Valdez
Director of Art Production _
Teresa Rad
Photographer _
David La Chapelle
Retoucher _
Stella Digital
Country _
USA

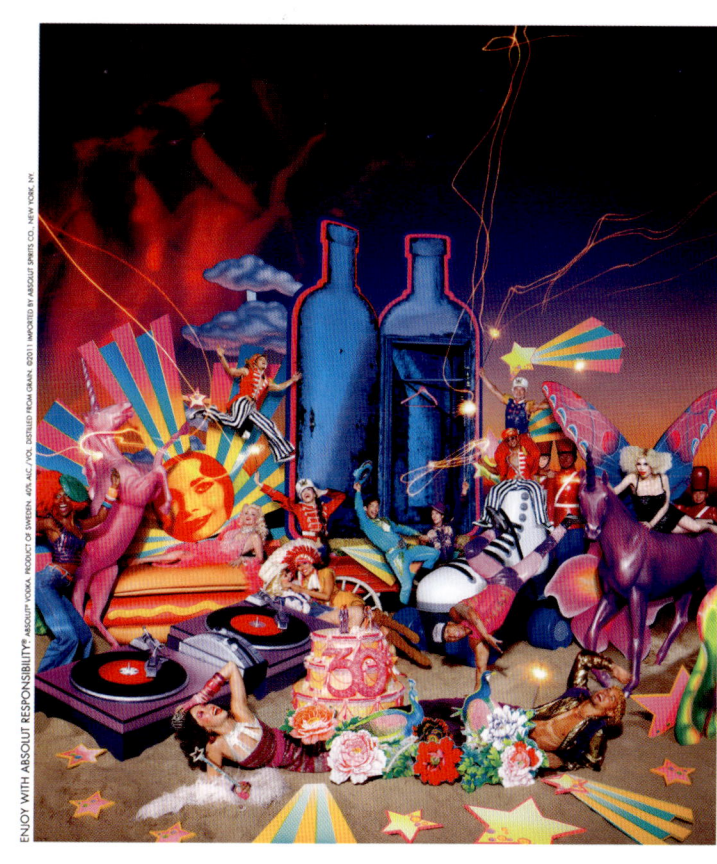

Client _
Infiniti
Studio _
TBWA/Chiat/Day
Chief Creative Officer _
Rob Schwartz
Creative Directors _
Bob Rayburn, Patrick Condo
Associate Creative Director _
John Figone
Copywriters _
Josh Stern, Chris DeNinno
Art Director _
Chase Madrid
Digital Associate Creative Director _
Ed Mun
Digital Designer _
Jose Eslinger
Artist _
Masako Inkyo
Country _
USA

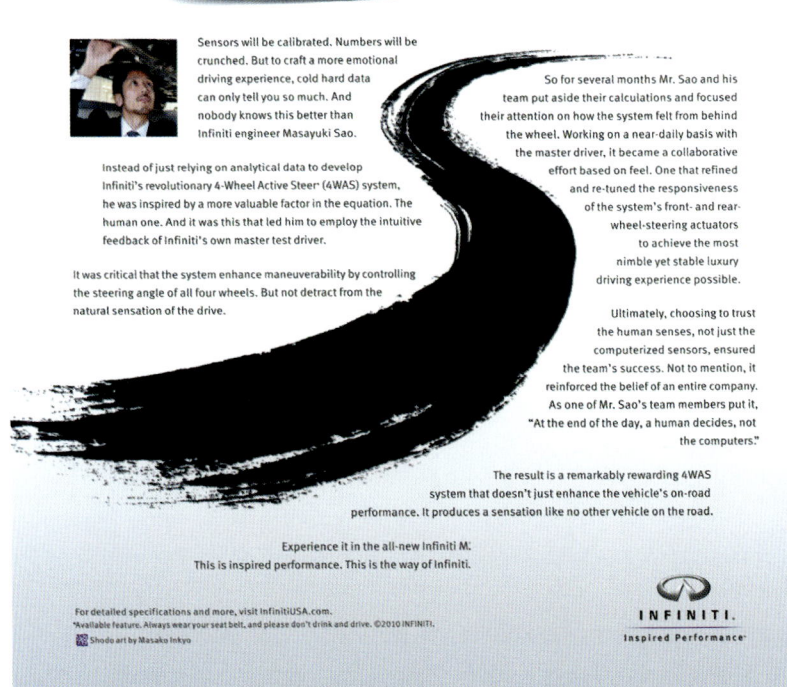

WAY OF INFINITI – M LAUNCH CAMPAIGN

The essence of every Infiniti is captured in two brush strokes of a shodo artist brush. Within them lie not only the design character of the vehicle, but the emotional experience the car is intended to create. TBWA/Chiat/Day has taken this ancient art form and modernised it into a series of shodo icons that represent the inspirations and features that make up each car. The idea is to create a contemporary visual language that instantly communicates the Infiniti brand. An iconic language that explains The Way Of Infiniti.

NO. 7
ON A HUMAN LEVEL

Better sound because of what you don't hear.

Client _
Swingkids
Studio _
Lundgren+Lindqvist
Photographer _
Cora Hillebrand
Country _
Sweden

NEW YEARS POSTER

New Year Poster 2008 summarising the year in terms of events, catastrophes, films, top brands (according to publicity and sales), artists, trends, new gadgets, influential people etc.

All of the 114 different illustrations were hand drawn and include:
Sarah Palin (as the hockey mom), Heath Ledger (RIP), Michael Phelps (8 gold medals, Beijing Olympics), Universal Studios (on fire – literally speaking), Vladimir Putin (resigning), Helvetica (the world's most famous typeface celebrating 50 years), Lehman Brothers (going down the drain), Isaac Hayes (as Chef, RIP), Mortage Crisis, Usain Bolt, Elmo (top selling toy Christmas 2008) to name a few.

We chose the Champagne bottle as an appropriate symbol for the New Year's Eve celebration.

Client _
Perrier Jouët
Agency _
Publicis Agency Paris
Creative Director _
Helene Kerbiquet/Publicis
Illustrator _
Jo Lynn Alcorn
Photographer _
Kanji Ishii
Country _
USA

PERRIER JOUËT CHAMPAGNE AD CAMPAIGN

I was commissioned by Publicis to make frescoes out of paper for Perrier Jouët, representing their 5 different cuvées. The aesthetic was based on the 1911 Belle Epoque bottle design of Emile Gallé.

Like a fine Champagne, a work of art in cut paper transforms Nature's organic elements into a crisp, delicate creation. Like Perrier Jouët, I draw on tradition, craft, and inspiration to create an aesthetic expression of the flow of life. I want to evoke Nature's beauty and life's harmony in a product that is materially ephemeral —but that creates a lasting, cherished memory.

Client _
Toyota España, Tiempo BBDO Madrid
Studio _
m Barcelona
Designer/ Illustrator _
Marion Dönneweg
Copywriter _
Alberto Jaén
Country _
Spain

TOYOTA

The new Toyota IQ is a very small 4-seater that competes with the Smart. Headlines: 4 seats, Less CO_2, 9 airbags, Rain Sensors, Fog Lamps, Touch Sreen, Shopping!

4 plazas.

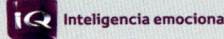

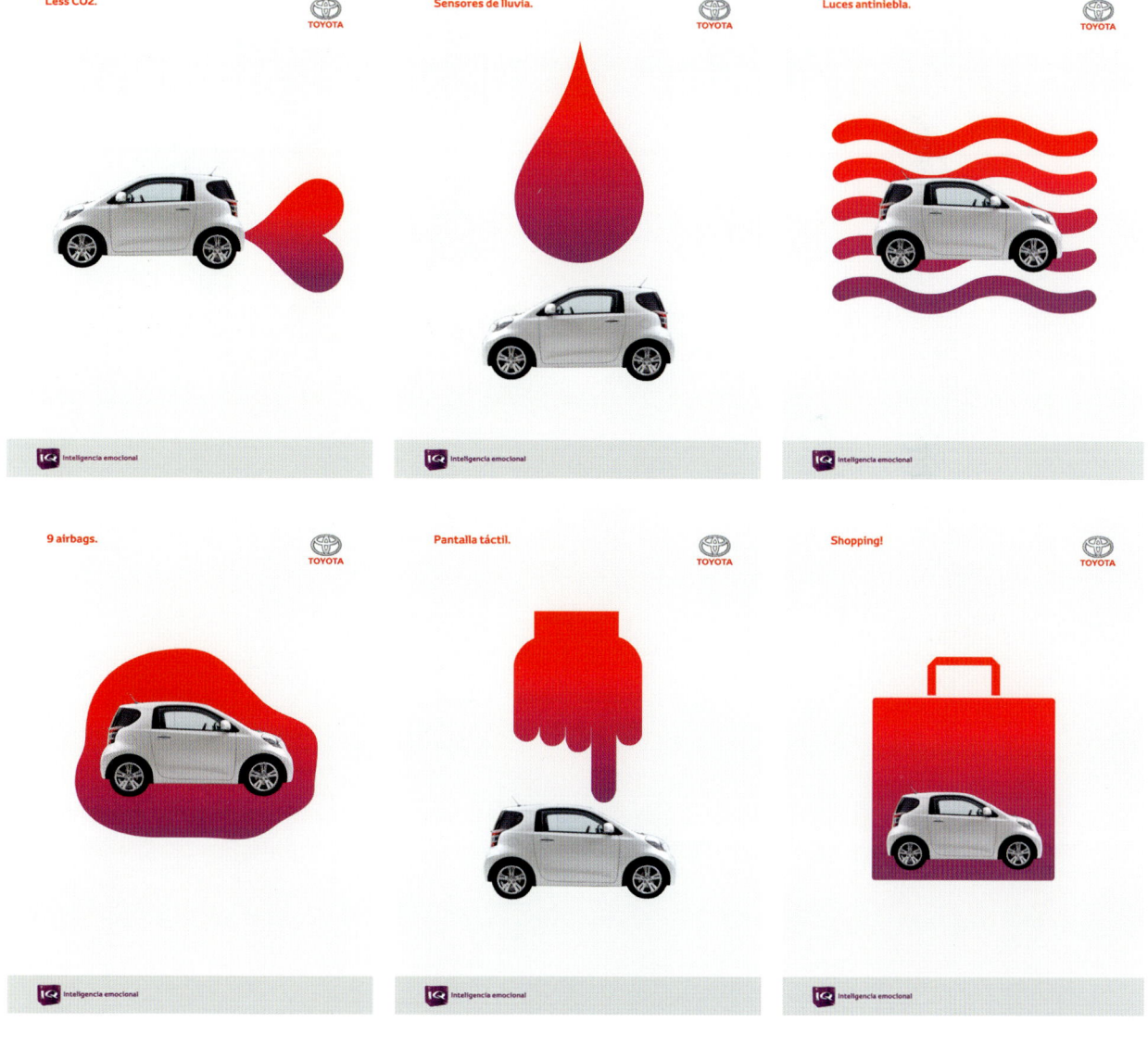

Client _
Gavin Martin Colournet
Studio _
Magpie Studio
Creative Directors _
David Azurdia, Ben Christie, Jamie Ellul
Designers _
Ben Christie, Tim Fellowes
Country _
UK

JOB BAGS

Having joined forces in 2010, Gavin Martin Associates and Colournet wanted to raise their new profile without breaking the joint bank account.
We suggested making use of an unused canvas — the humble proof bag. Used by printers to deliver wet proofs to their clients, the bags were screen printed with a life-sized collection of eccentric objects.
Tucked under the arm, the proof bags act as walking billboards en route, and a talking point when dropped off. Low cost, high impact and the promise of raising a smile.

Client _
Billy Blue School of Design
Studio _
Motherbird
Country _
Australia

BILLY BLUE SCHOOL OF DESIGN

Billy Blue School of Design recently opened a campus in Melbourne, and Motherbird were commissioned to produce a campaign noting this arrival. Our hand-made paper shape scenes were based around the 3 Billy Blue values — Thinking, Making & Connecting. The tagline "Adventure into Design" played a large part in the way we developed these visuals.

Client _
Houdini Sydney/Euro RSCG
Studio _
Rudi de Wet Studio
Creative Director _
Warrick Nicholson
Art Director _
Adrian McNamara
Country _
South Africa

CLEARASIL DREAMS

Cinema Media Campaign.

Client _
Atomik
Studio _
POGO
Creative Director _
Ardi Carlos Grygierzcyk
Art Director _
Pauli Filippelli
Designer _
Guillermo Vizzari
Illustrator _
Pauli Filippelli
Photographer _
Cecilia Glik
Country _
Argentina

ATOMIK FALL WINTER CAMPAIGN 2011

For this campaign we recreated an illustrated environment representing the daily life of young kids.

Client _
Turkish Airlines
Studio _
RDB CG
Creative Director _
Tuğhan Garip
Art Directors _
Tolga Oruç, Mehmet Emre Mutlu
Copywriters _
Selin Hamamciyan, Çaglar Alkaya
Country _
Turkey

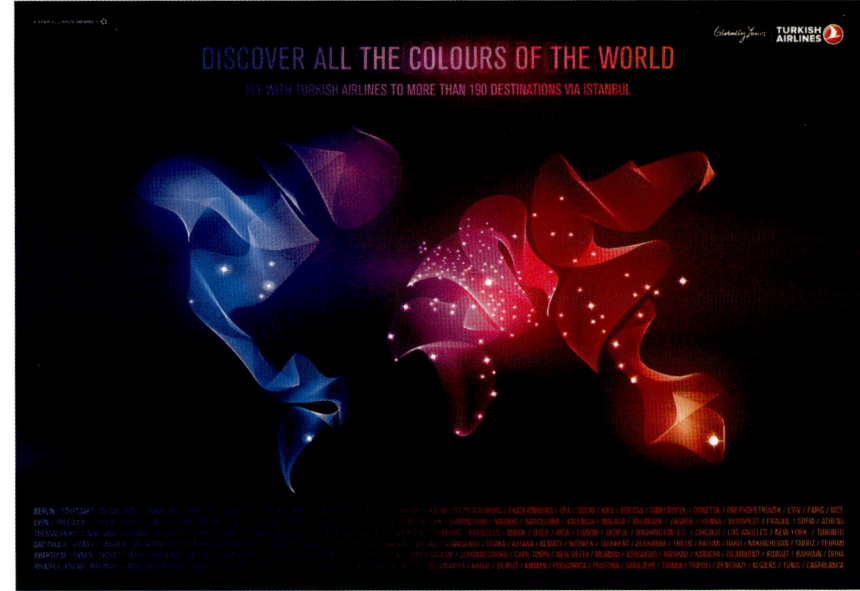

TURKISH AIRLINES: NETWORK MAPS

Turkish Airlines, one of the world's fastest growing air carriers, is continually expanding its quota of destinations. Our brief was to create a striking print and billboard campaign that highlighted the fact that Turkish Airlines now offers its customers more international connections than ever before. We aimed to create work that was visually arresting with minimal copy. We wanted our message to be communicated through the visuals as much as possible.

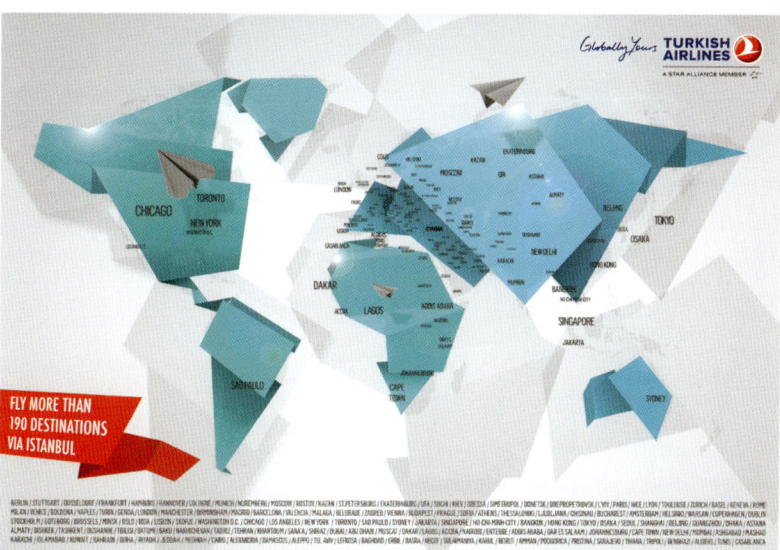

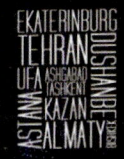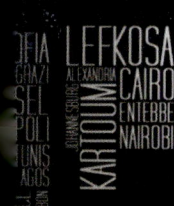

Client _
Berliner Philharmonie GmbH
Agency _
Scholz & Friends Berlin
Creative Directors _
Michael Winterhagen, Nils Busche, Matthias Spaetgens
Art Director _
Philipp Weber
Copywriter _
Felix John
Designers _
Lisa Baur, Robert Bilz, Klaus Bornhöft, Stefanie Busse, Dominika Dobrzalski, Marc Ebenwaldner, Björn Ewers, Juan Gonzalez, Ralph Haas, Daniel Hahn, Florian Hucker, Lina Jachmann, Christoph Keller, Heidrun Kleingries, Antonia Leven, Maja Mack, Miguel Martinez, Andrew Morgan, Susanne Peters, Anatolij Pickmann, Yvonne Rutten, Luis Sanchez, Theresa Scholz, Lisa-Marie Schröder, Jens Stein, Roman Schultze, Esther Schwarz, Sebastian Tost, Antje von Daniels, Walter Ziegler
Photographer _
Hans Stark
Consulting _
Katrin Seegers, Katja Weiden, Sonja Overbeck
Country _
Germany

128 STARS – 1 ORCHESTRA

The Berlin Philharmonic is one of the best orchestras in the world. Nonetheless, the big performances are mostly sold out, while the small ensemble concerts are not. The brief was to communicate in a unique and unseen way that it's the individual members who give the whole orchestra its exceptional quality. So that the orchestra's excellent reputation also reflects on the individual musicians and their smaller concerts.
The campaign presents all members of the Berlin Philharmonic as what they are: real stars. For every one of the 128 musicians, an individual poster was designed. The posters were spread on billboards around Berlin, without any further comment. After two weeks, it was disclosed that together they are the Berlin Philharmonic. The poster motifs were also featured in the season preview, the website and on city-light posters.

Who are they?

After two weeks: the disclosure.

Client _
Army Museum
Agency _
SILO
Creative Director _
Rene Toneman
Designers _
Scott Savage, Eline Wieriks, Rene Toneman
Country _
The Netherlands

KNIGHTS TOURNAMENT

Ready for the fight? For "Tournament Knights", Silo designed the promotional campaign. Children and adults transport themselves back to the Middle Ages during a festive jousting tournament. Put on a helmet, feel the weight of a sword, or pull back a cross-bow. For those who dare: take your place on a tournament horse and dress up for the competition.
Silo developed a concept based on the highly decorative and fantasy-rich visual language from the time period: Heraldry. The presentation of knight-on-horse functions as a public declaration. The illustration is constructed entirely out of colour paper then photographed. Based on this concept, the Military Museum decided to host a contest for the best construction-paper knight.

ROMAN RETURN TICKET

Discover how life would have been as a Roman soldier! For the program "Roman return ticket" Silo designed a promotional campaign about life as a Roman soldier. Children aged 6 to 10 will explore in a playful way how Roman soldiers lived while serving in the territory which became The Netherlands. Silo developed a concept to photograph children dressed up in Roman soldier uniforms are made of kitchen utensils and home supplies (amongst dad's record collection). It communicates the rich fantasy of children concerning the subject, and visualises a great visit to the Army Museum for all the family. The uniforms are accurately created, based on three different types of soldiers and ranks.

Client _
Army Museum
Agency _
SILO
Creative Director _
Rene Toneman
Designer _
Rene Toneman
Photographer _
Nadine Stijns
Styling _
Daniela Larue
Country _
The Netherlands

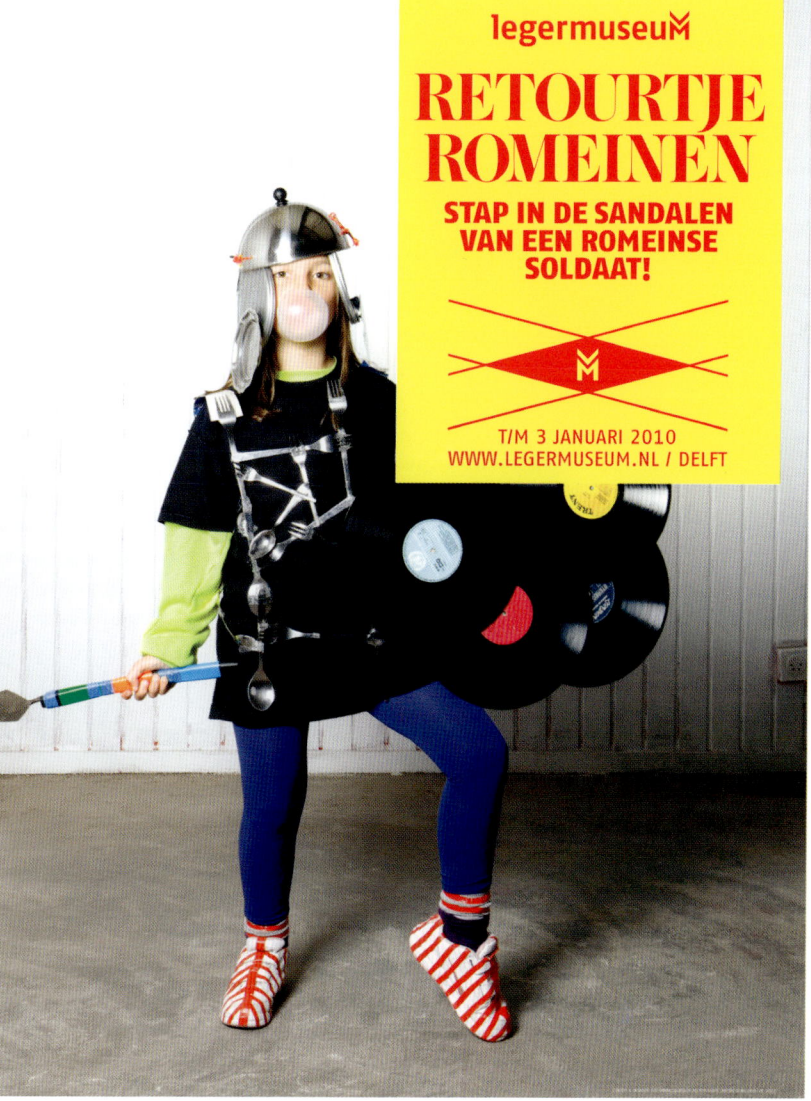

Client _
Utrecht City Theatre
Agency _
EDENSPIEKERMANN AMSTERDAM
Creative Director _
Edo van Dijk
Photographer _
Gerrit Schreurs
Country _
Country

UTRECHT CITY THEATRE'S NEW CULTURAL SEASON

Edenspiekermann is a leading international design agency with offices in Amsterdam, Stuttgart and Berlin. Edenspiekermann designs brand experiences, starting with a strategy, choosing the appropriate medium to deliver it and then designing the complete experience.

Every year, the Utrecht City Theatre and Edenspiekermann invite a guest artist — photographer or illustrator — to develop a series of images that react on the two brand identity keywords "reflective" and "scintillating".

For the 2010/2011 cultural season, we invited Dutch photographer Gerrit Schreurs to create a series of images that would enrich the visual identity of the theatre during the upcoming year. These images are used in the season programme booklet as dividing pages between the various programme themes. They are then are combined by the artist into collages in the outdoor and online campaign that introduces the new cultural season.

Client _
Evergreen
Studio _
zig
Executive Creative Director _
Martin Beauvais
Art Director _
Mark Puchala
Copywriter _
Geoff Morgan
Planner _
James Powell
Team Leader _
Christine Harron
Team Leader _
Christine Harron
Agency Producer _
Christine Harron
Print Producer _
Jen Dark/Darcy Paniccia
Photographer _
Matt Barnes - Westside Studios
Film House _
247 Integrated/zig
Retoucher _
Matt Barnes, Jeremy Thompson
Country _
Canada

EVERGREEN

zig, an ideas company within the MDC Partners network, created the "Be the Root" marketing campaign for Evergreen, the national not-for-profit campaign to promote its grassroots approach to introducing and preserving nature in an urban setting. The campaign was launched in April 2009 and was created to raise national awareness for Evergreen and to drive a sense of community by getting Canadians involved in initiating and sustaining nature in their cities. The campaign targeted Canadians who live in urban spaces across the country and who know that nature is important but don't fully understand the benefits or what they can do.

IKEA HOLIDAY CAMPAIGN

IKEA Canada partnered with ZIG, an agency of record, in December 2008 to launch a marketing campaign to showcase its ability to help people create cosy and festive homes for the holidays. The campaign focused on the importance of preparing a home for the holiday season rather than gift giving. Using only items that are available in IKEA stores, zig created imagery for out-of-home and online advertising that spells out traditional holiday messages and showcases the unique items available for the season.

Client _
IKEA Canada
Studio _
zig
Executive Creative Director _
Martin Beauvais
Art Director _
Mark Puchala
Copywriter _
Geoff Morgan
Coach _
Shelley Brown
Planner _
Mark Aronson
Team Leader _
Lesley Rivard
Project Manager _
Hailey Anevich
Photographer _
Matt Barnes
Country _
Canada

Client _
The Zimbabween Newspaper
Studio _
TBWA Hunt Lascaris
Account Director _
Bridget Langley
Account Director _
Bridget Langley
Copywriters _
Raphael Basckin, Nicholas Hulley
Art Directors _
Shelley Smoler, Nadja Lossgott
Photographers _
Chloe Coetsee, Des Ellis, Rob Wilson
Creative Directors _
Nicholas Hulley, Damon Stapleton
Executive Creative Director_
John Hunt
Country_
South Africa

ZIMBABWEAN

Our client, The Zimbabwean newspaper, has been driven into exile for reporting on how the Mugabe regime has rigged elections, crushed the opposition, caused poverty, disease and the total collapse of the economy. And now, having exiled them, the regime has slapped a 55% luxury import duty on the paper (as if freedom of speech is a luxury) that makes it unaffordable for the average Zimbabwean.

To get the paper into Zimbabwean hands, it needs to be subsidized, and our client can only do that by raising awareness and driving sales outside Zimbabwe.

We developed a unique solution. One of the most eloquent symbols of Zimbabwe's collapse is the Z$ trillion dollar note, a symptom of their world record inflation. This banknote, and the dizzying escalation of notes that has preceded it, cannot buy anything, not even a loaf of bread — and certainly not any advertising.

But it can become the advertising. So, we turned the money into its own medium.

We took this useless currency, cheaper than paper, and printed our messages all over it. Overnight, trillions of dollars of Zimbabwe note, achieved what they'd never been able to buy — real and meaningful advertising coverage. Within hours, we were in the national press. And a couple of days later, the campaign was on national television and radio. And then the Internet discovered it and it spread across the world.

Soon we were on the New York Times site, Yahoo news, the Huffington Post, other news sites and hundreds and hundreds of websites and blogs. As the campaign continues, sales of The Zimbabwean continue to soar.

In the week of the roll-out alone, the website logged over 2 million hits. Sales increased by 276% and more copies of The Zimbabwean than ever are crossing the border into Zimbabwe.

We used Mugabe's own creation against him.

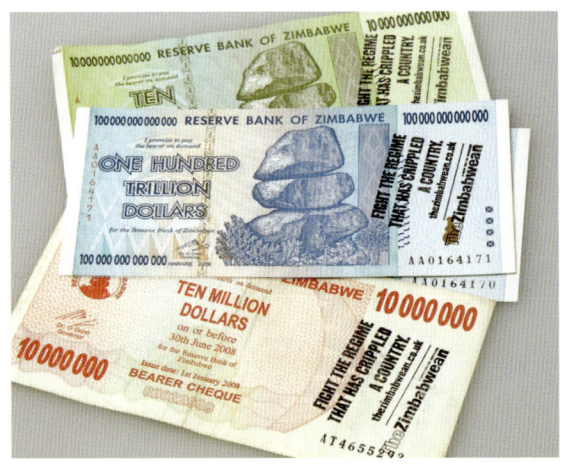

Client _
SISO
Studio _
Zoo Studio
Creative Director _
Gerard Calm
Designer _
Xavier Castells
Photographer _
Ivan Raga
Country _
Spain

ARTABAC 2011

Educational campaign directed at "Osona" schools.

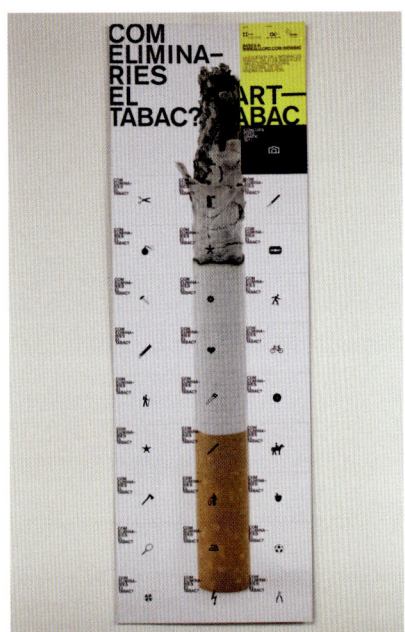
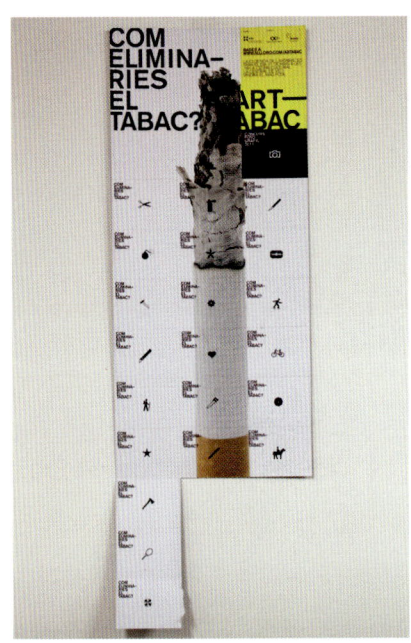
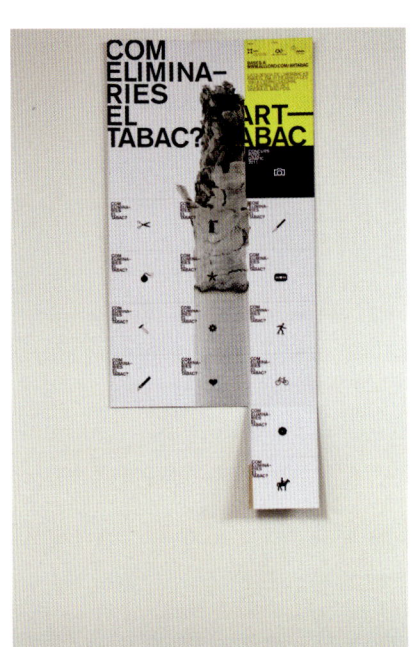
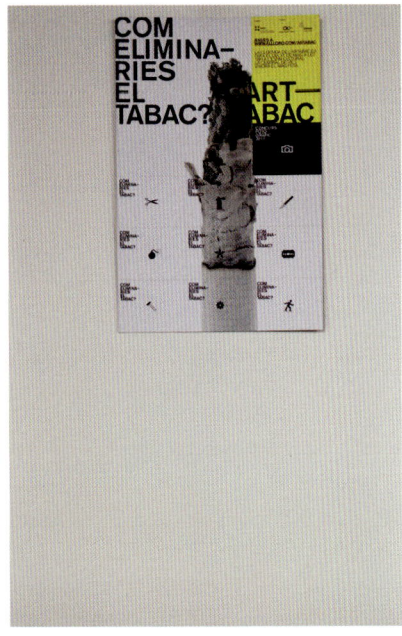
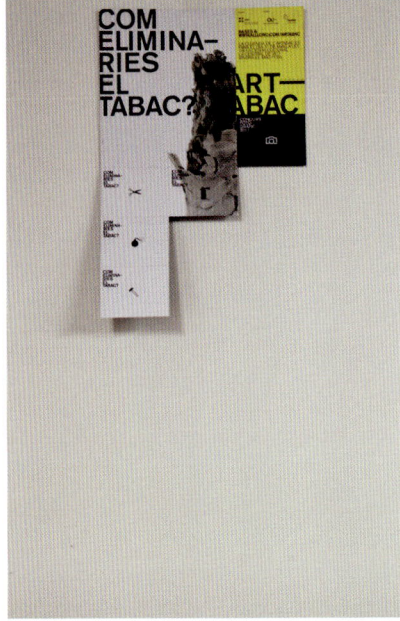

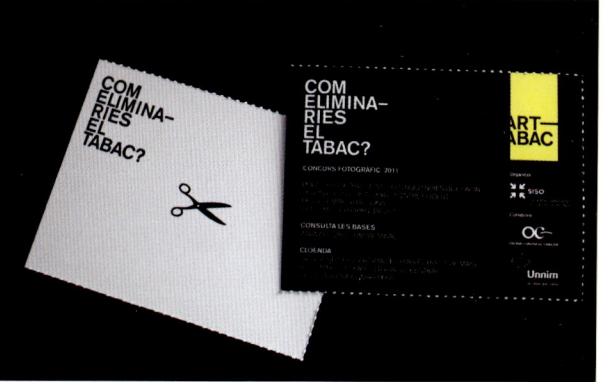

CAMPAIGN | 97

Client _
AMRRIC
Agency _
GHG Australia
Creative Director _
Tim Brierley
Art Director _
Daragh Ledwidge
Copywriters _
Daragh Ledwidge, Tim Brierley
Designer _
Daragh Ledwidge (logo)
Photographer _
David Knight
Account Manager _
Patricia Crimmins
Country _
Australia

ULURUFF

The challenge was to raise awareness about AMRRIC (Animal Management in Rural and Remote Indigenous Communities) with a fresh campaign and a new brand identity. AMRRIC is a not-for-profit organisation that provides essential healthcare to indigenous community pets; they also educate indigenous Australians on how to look after their pets.

To inspire support for AMRRIC's ideals, our creative approach highlights connections between indigenous Australians, their land and their pets. This insight informs AMRRIC's print and TV ad, and their new logo. All our work for AMRRIC is pro bono.

AMRRIC's new brand identity and print ads have met with considerable acclaim by both pet health professionals and our client. Our print ad appears in the Australian Veterinary Journal, and across AMMRIC's awareness collateral. The new TVC is due to air mid-2012.

CATALOGUE
BROCHURE
LEAFLET

Client _
Jonathan Ellery/Mulberry
Studio _
Browns
Creative Director _
Jonathan Ellery
Designers _
Jonathan Ellery, Sabrina Grill
Country _
UK

WORLDLY CARES AND LOVE AFFAIRS

In Autumn 2010, Jonathan Ellery was commissioned by Mulberry to produce a sculptural piece for their new flagship store at 50 New Bond Street in London. The piece consists of 25 circular, machined, solid brass pieces which have been embedded into the concrete floor of the store at specific locations.
The catalogue shows the sequential narrative and reveals where the pieces can be found within the store at 50 New Bond Street.

Client _
Calle
Studio _
Hort
Country _
Germany

CALLE BRAND NEWSPRINT

Promotional brand-newsprint for Calle.
Part of the lookbook we designed for the Bread & Butter fair.

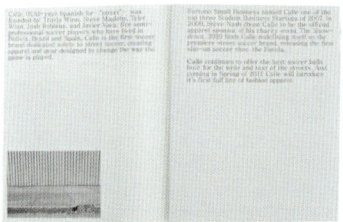

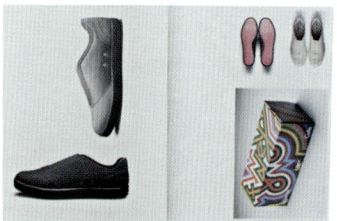

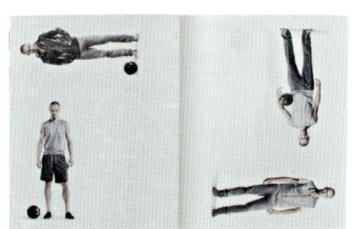

Client _
DEAG Music GmbH
Studio _
Hort
Country _
Germany

ZPYZ

Art direction and design for the band ZPYZ, including all releases and all promotional materials.

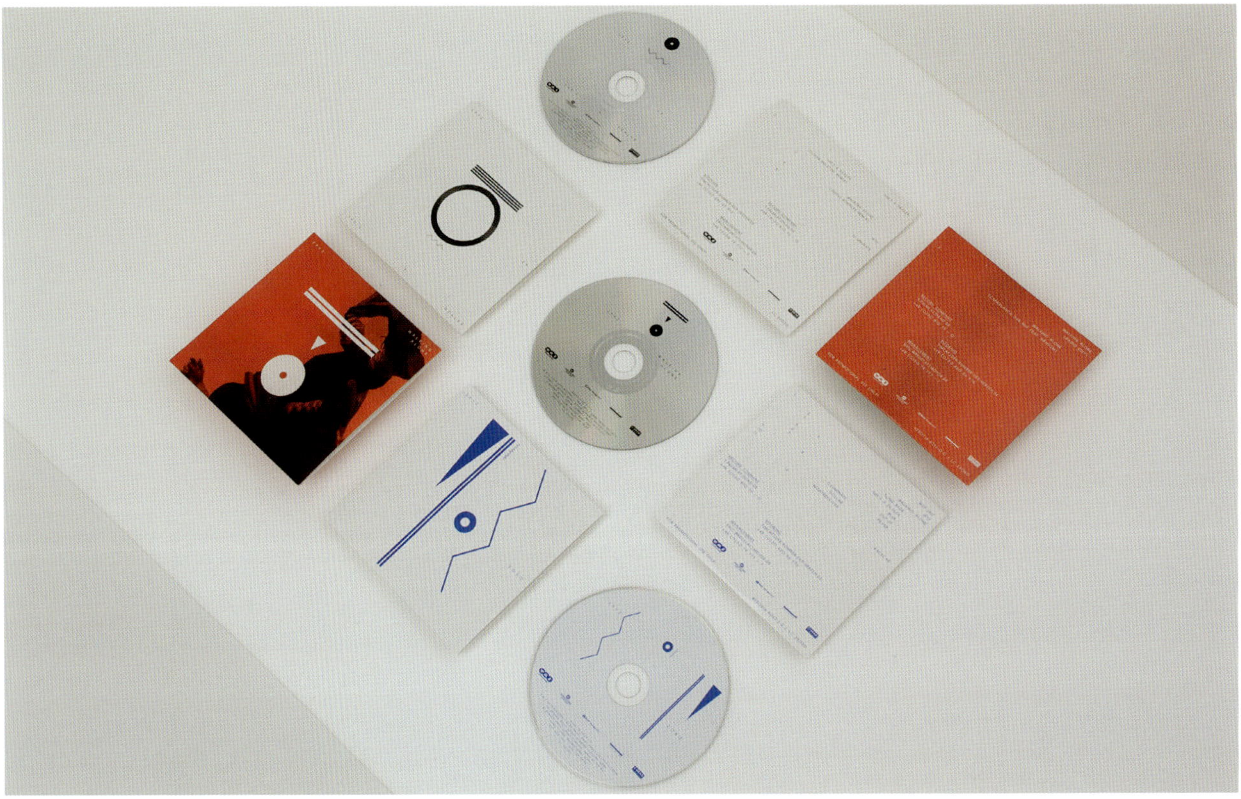

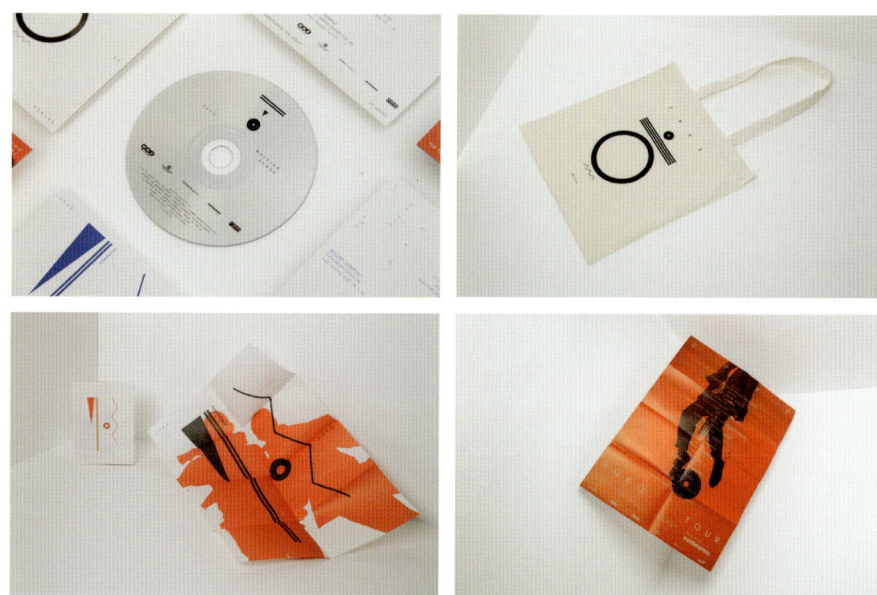

CATALOGUE, BROCHURE, LEAFLET | 105

Studio _
ilovedust
Country _
UK

ILOVEDUST BLACK BOOK

ilovedust wanted to design an eye-catching promotional piece to showcase its latest work, so the "black book" was born!
It contains a collection of its recent artwork, from global projects undertaken for Nike and Kiehl's, to smaller projects on behalf of local independent companies that we support in our local community. The book was presented in unique die-cut, gold-foiled slipcase, with a combination of gold and black foil stamps to create a fresh, innovative design.

Studio _
Bunch
Country _
Croatia

BUNCH OF STARS

The project evolved from Bunch being chosen to devise a distinct identity for The Star of Bethnal Green in 2008. A traditional long-tailed star was taken and illustrated to create artwork that represented the corresponding month. This was applied each month for approximately a year with all of the illustration done in house by Bunch.
Illustrators were then sought out from the furthest reaches of the globe including Guatemala, Iceland, Uganda and Indonesia to celebrate and explore the concept of how stars appear differently depending on where in the world you happen to be.
Bunch of Stars brochure, limited edition screen-printed poster and t-shirts are exclusively available from our online shop.

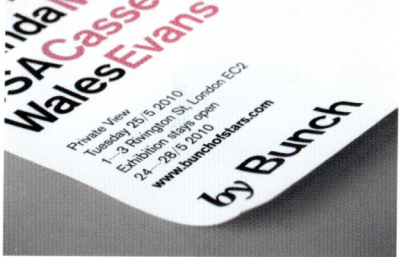

CATALOGUE, BROCHURE, LEAFLET

Client _
Vermelho Gallery
Studio _
Campo
Creative Directors/Art directors/Designers _
Paula Tinoco, Carolina Aboarrage
Photographer _
Rafael Assef
Country _
Germany

VERBO 2010

Verbo is an annual performance festival produced by Vermelho Gallery, São Paulo, since 2002. The studio developed the identity for the festival based on diagonal lines, and year by year, this concept is revisited in different ways, always under the idea of movement.

For this year, we made a brochure and a modular piece that serves as a schedule poster and also like the signage of the exhibition. Around 60 of these posters were displayed on a wall at the entrance of the exhibition, side by side, forming a colorful pattern.

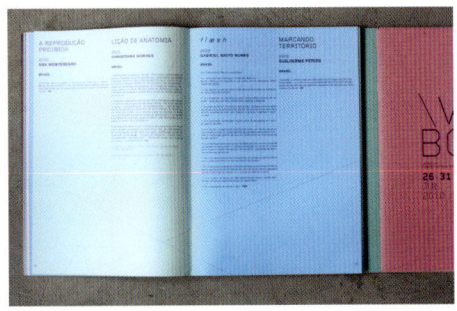

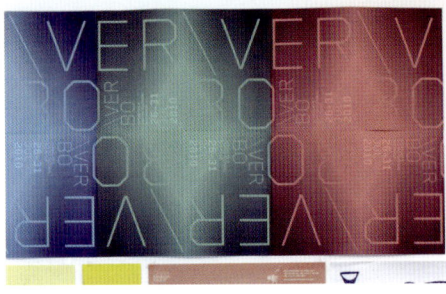

Client _
ICEX (Spanish Institute for Foreign Trade) , Spanish National Association of Furniture Exporters
Studio _
Estudio Ibán Ramón
Country _
Spain

ENJOY YOUR KITCHEN

Fold-up poster with a large, semi-perforated card inside that itself can be divided up into 12 cards. Promotional piece for international markets by the Spanish kitchen furniture industry.

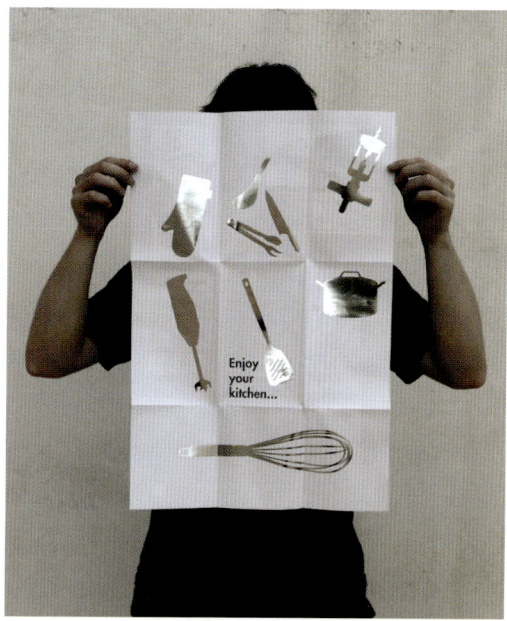
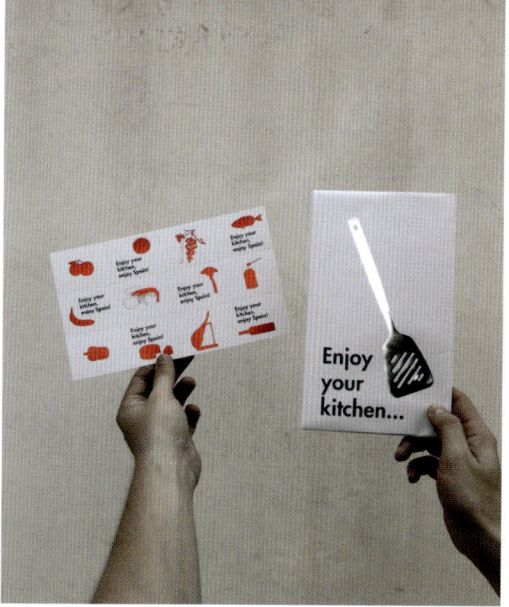

Client _
University of Patras, Greece
Studio _
G Design Studio
Creative Directors _
Alexandros Gavrilakis, Michalis Georgiou
Art Director _
Diamantis Arabatzis
Photographer _
Yiannis Aesopos
Editor _
Yiannis Aesopos
Country _
Greece

10TH ANNIVERSARY IDENTITY FOR DEPARTMENT OF ARCHITECTURE

We were commissioned to design the identity for the 10th anniversary celebration of the Department of Architecture, University of Patras.
The number 10 is depicted through geometrical shapes that refer to the department's objectives while the very same shapes were used to create numerous patterns for various applications.
Special paper for the outer case, fluorescent & golden pantone for the guide itself, numerous paper qualities and a distinctive bonding form an exceptional outcome.
The "golden" anniversary poster was designed blending photos illustrating student life of the last decade. Also included in the 2010 course catalogue.

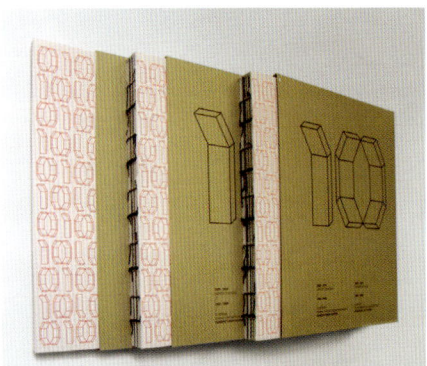

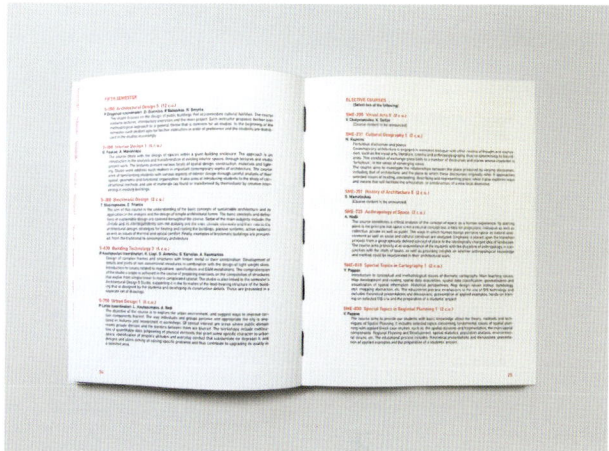

CATALOGUE, BROCHURE, LEAFLET | 113

Client _
Tipos Libres
Studio _
Wonksite Studio
Creative Director/Art Director/Designer _
Jorge Restrepo
Countr _
Colombia

DH14

Dejando Huella is one of the most important festival around the design in Mexico. The conference join around 1,500 designers of all regions from México, and really is a party with an excuse, the design.
To this version I was commissioned to create the brand of the event, I was thinking about the name: Dejando Huella (Set trend) is a Spanish expression that means to give a mark in the people but in addition, Dejando Huella means walk step by step. I use a couple of legs running, with some emblematic palette of color in my works, with a analogue type. The idea really was to create an image simple, impact and contemporary.

Client _
Colombiage Festival
Creative DirectorArt Director/Designer _
Jorge Restrepo
Copywriter _
Landa Scott
Country _
Colombia

COLOMBIAGE

The UK's most influential celebration of contemporary Colombian arts and culture. Colombiage was launched in 2007 with the aim of showing the rest of the world the diversity of Colombian culture while giving birth to a creative platform of intercultural exchange between Colombia and the UK. The festival was conceived as 'collage' of talent, art forms and audiences; an alternative space for stimulating dialogues between Colombia and the UK, a space that would inspire new types of collaboration, encounters and discoveries. I was commissioned to create the image for Colombiage 2010 at London. The idea was to create a collage of elements around the butterflies with birds flying in the compositión. In addition, we created a postcard to Manu Chao's opening concert.

Client _
Michell 1870
Studio _
Mash
Designer _
Darren Hock Guan Song
Art Director _
Dom Roberts
Country _
Australia

MICHELL YARN PROMO BROCHURE

As a sub brand of Michell 1870, Michell Yarn provides yarn to other fabric makers. This is the treated raw material used to make wool fabrics. A new brand was created that tied in closely with the Michell 1870 sister brand. Using the same unique typeface developed by Mash, a simple printed concertina brochure was created which reflected the quality and technological nature of Michell Yarn. This printed piece served to introduce and communicate the features and benefits of the product. One colour printing on a specialty uncoated paper with environmental credentials brought the geometric interpretations of the yarn spindle to life.

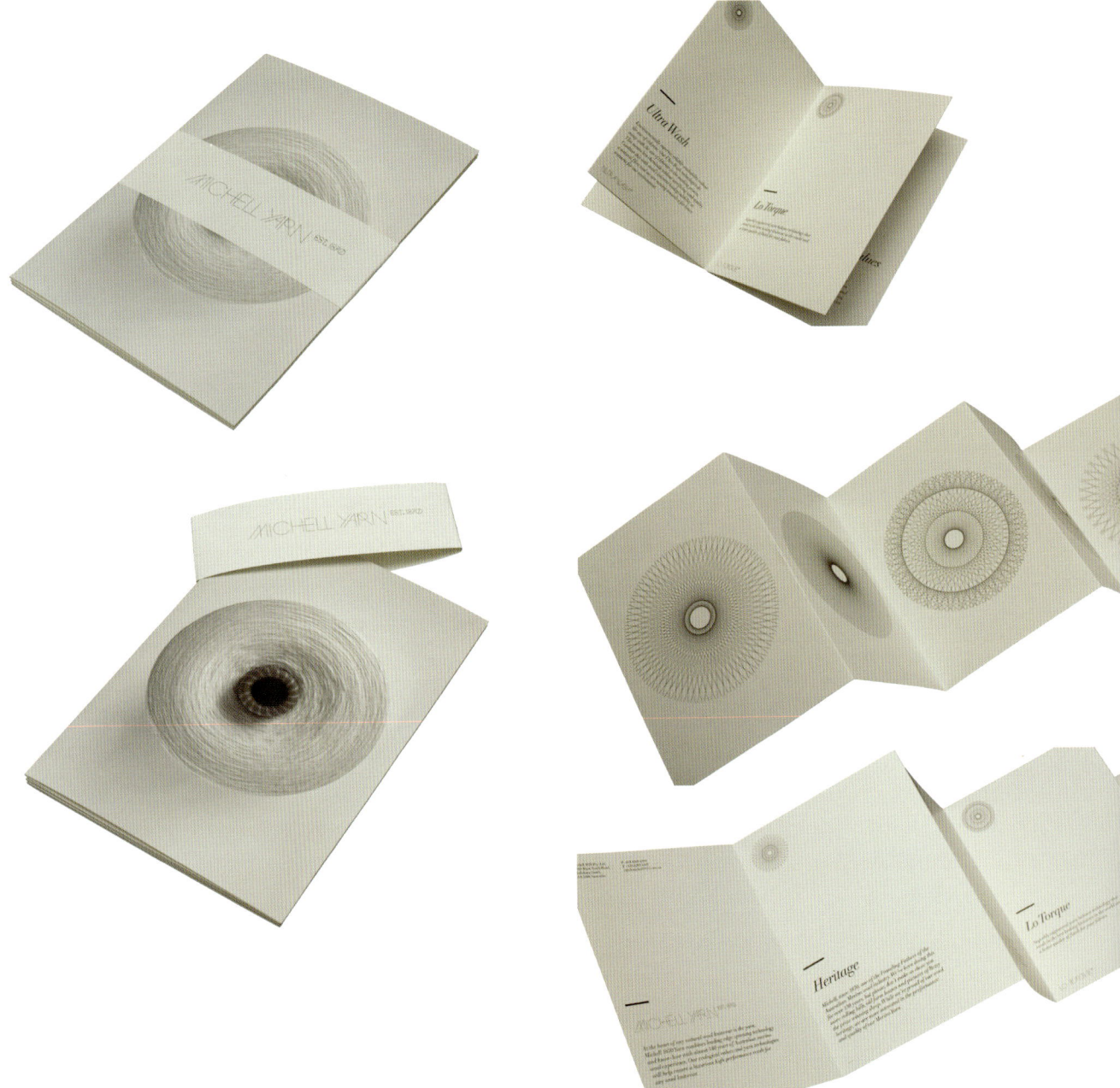

RESTAURANT HINDENBURG

Hindenburg Brochure is issued by Ginderdur restaurant quarterly. It's dedicated to remarkable events of the past and present of airship building. The main aim of the brochure is to entertain and educate the client of the restaurant.

Client _
Restaurant Hindenburg
Designer _
Pitertsev Mikhail
Country _
Russia

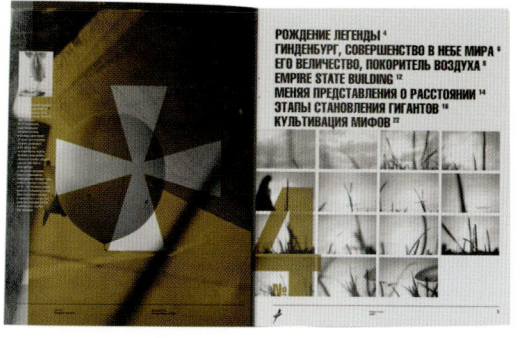
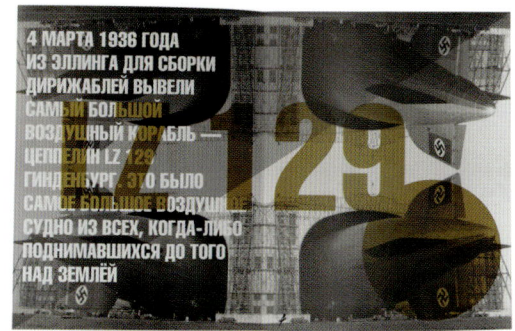
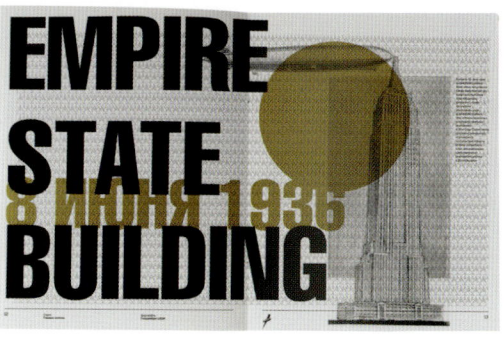
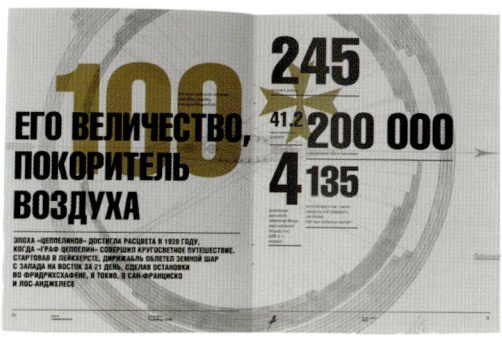

Client _
Associação Moda Lisboa
Studio _
Musa Work Lab
Country _
Portugal

ESTORIL FASHION ART FESTIVAL

Corporate identity, brand system and visual development for Estoril Art and Fashion annual festival 2010, organized by Moda Lisboa to promote tourism on the Estoril coast.

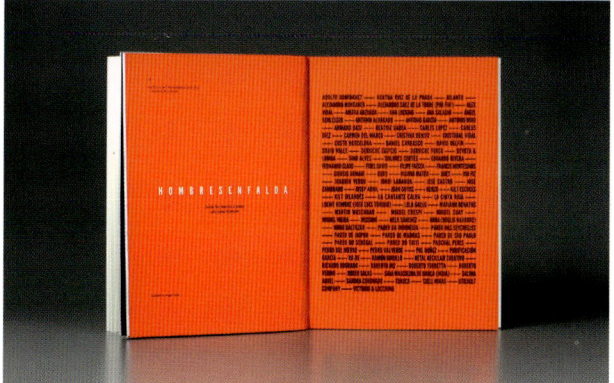

CATALOGUE, BROCHURE, LEAFLET | 121

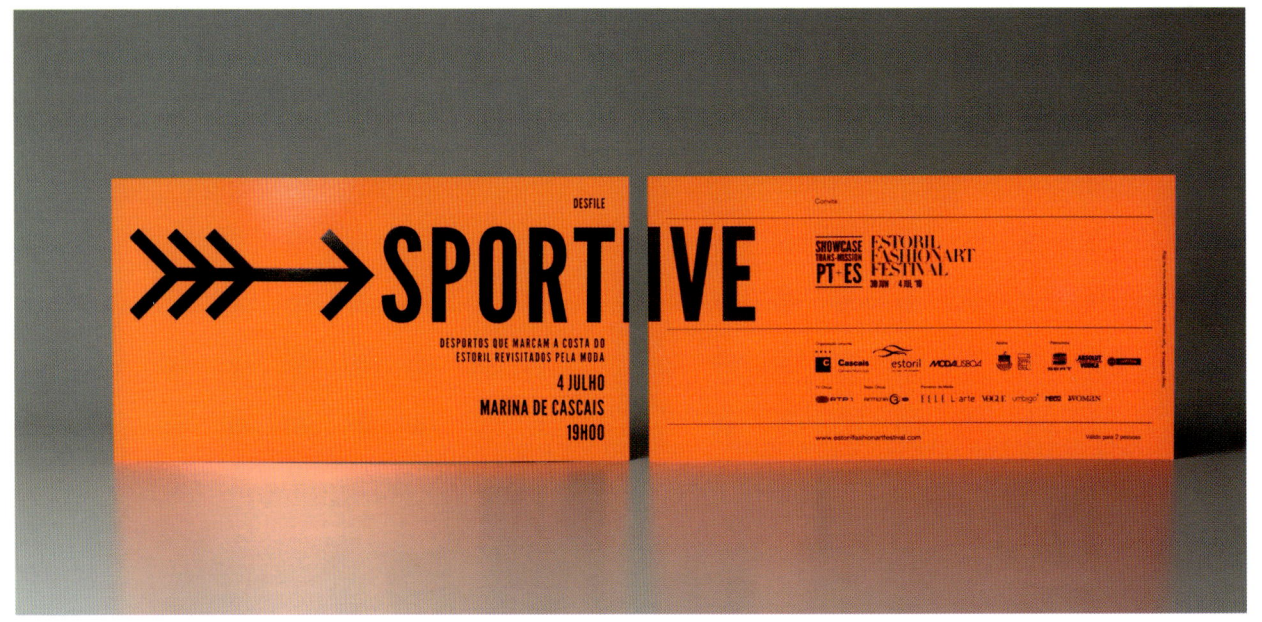

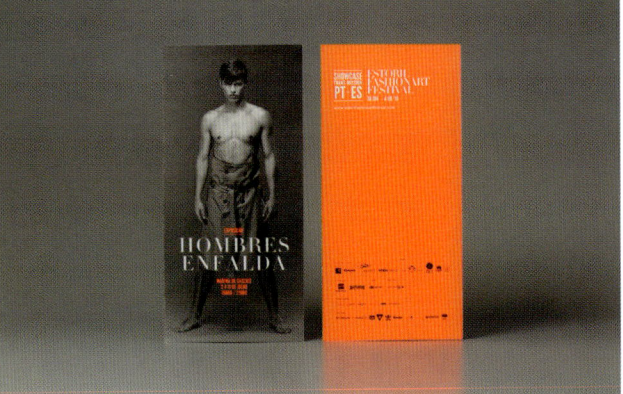

CATALOGUE, BROCHURE, LEAFLET

CATALOGUE, BROCHURE, LEAFLET

Client _
Moda Lisboa
Studio _
Musa Work Lab
Country _
Portugal

CHECK POINT

"Check Point" was the theme of the 34th edition of the Lisbon Fashion Week. All parts created as flyers, designer invitations, party invitations, the little newspaper, were based on a very simple language based only on a type and combination of colour. The numbering was used as a high graphical element that also worked very well the level of organisation of contents and order of the show.

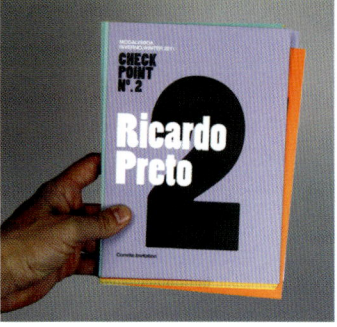

PAUL WEEKS PROMO

  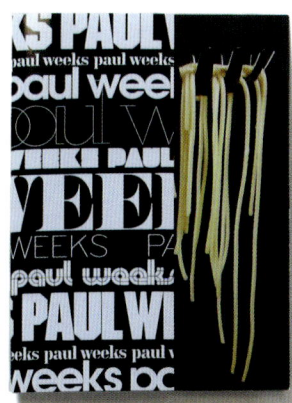 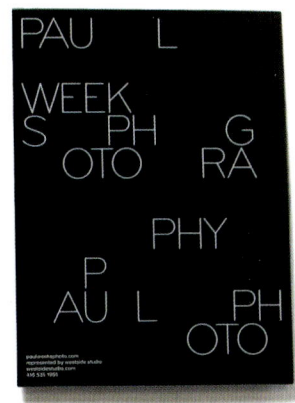

Studio _
Underline Studio
Art Directors _
Fidel Pena, Claire Dawson
Designer _
Claire Dawson
Photographer _
Paul Weeks
Country _
Canada

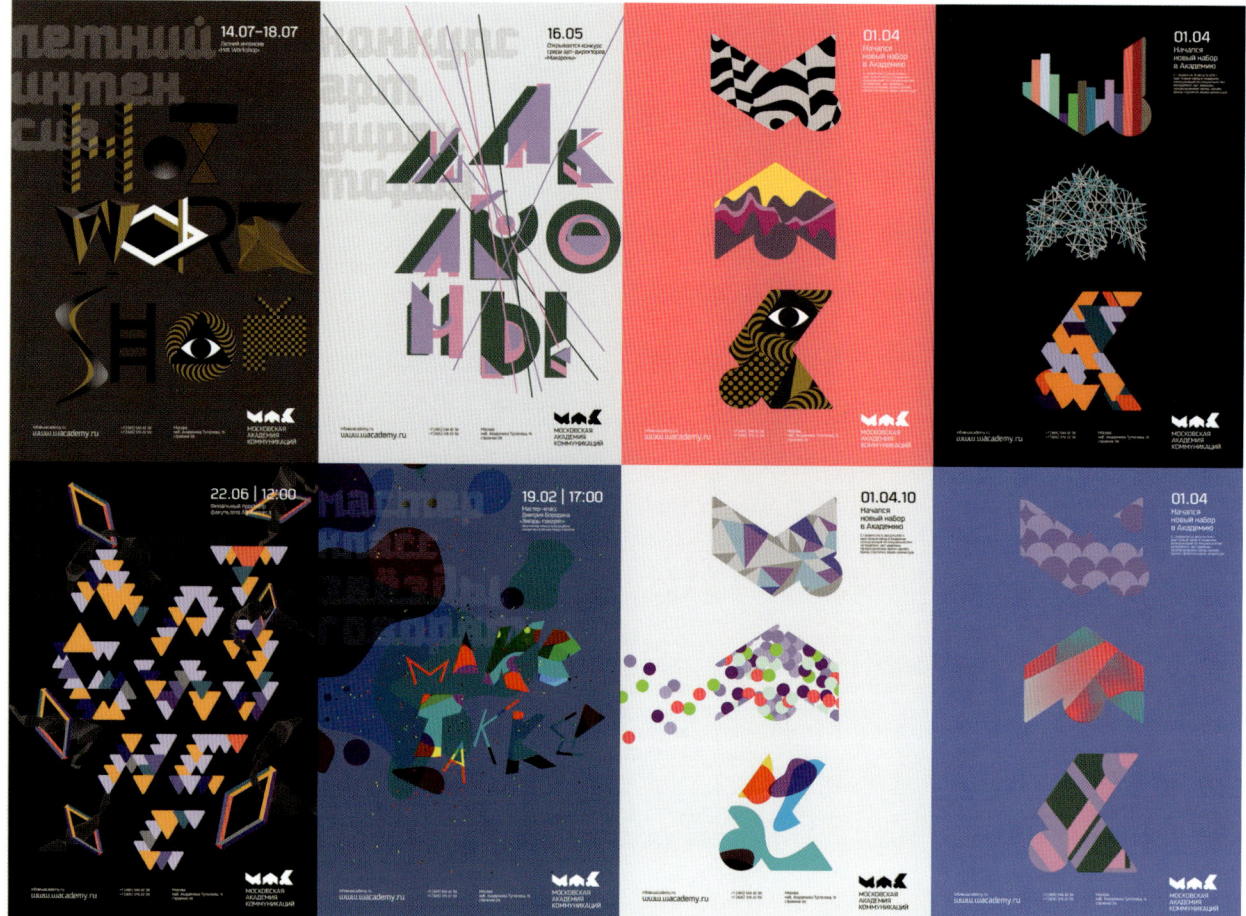

Client _
BHSAD

Designer _
Pitertsev Mikhail

Country _
Russia

MAK

MAK (Moscow Communication Academy) is new generation educational institution, which trains new staff for the communication industry. The Academy combines a university, creative studio, master classes, and professional community.

CATALOGUE, BROCHURE, LEAFLET

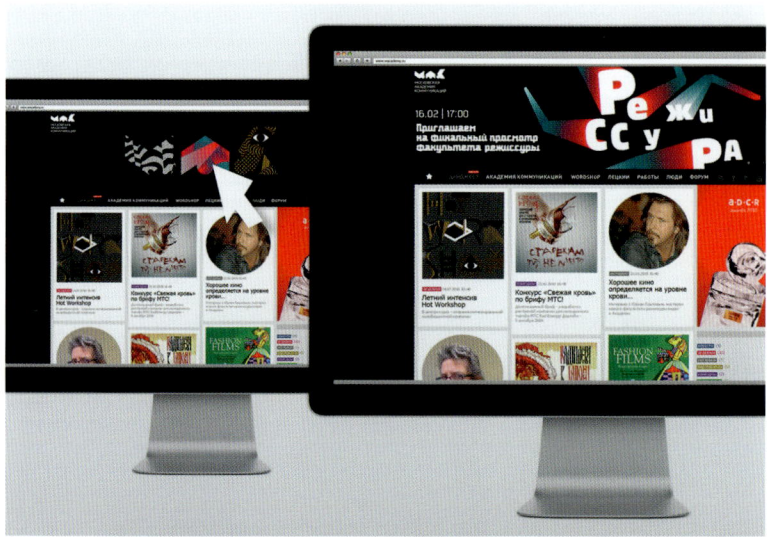

Client _
Barefoot Productions
Studio _
Program Studio
Designer _
Chris May
Country _
USA

TWENTY FOUR

Barefoot Productions is a Chicago based collaborative of artists, dancers and entertainers. I was asked to create the promotional materials for their annual staging of 24. In the production, the participants have 24 hours to create, rehearse and edit a performance to be staged immediately thereafter. Thankfully, I was allowed a bit more time to develop the campaign.

Client _
City of Port Phillip
Studio _
Studio Brave
Creative Director _
Tim Sutherland
Designers _
Elise Lampe, Katrina Tesoriero
Country _
Australia

ST KILDA FESTIVAL 2011

The St Kilda Festival is Melbourne's biggest summer outdoor event. The 9-day live music festival embraces Australian talent, Indigenous culture, performers and artists.

Client _
Foundation Rwanda
Agency _
JWT | Atlanta
Creative Director _
Carl Warner
Art Director _
Jeff Harter
Copywriter _
David Cohen
Illustrator _
Tom Janousek
Photographer _
Brad Kaye
Project Manager _
George Medland
Country _
USA

CHANGING PERSPECTIVES | CHANGING FUTURES

THE TRAGEDY

In 1994, an estimated 800,000 Rwandans were massacred in 100 days, thousands of women were raped, and an estimated 20,000 children were born from these rapes.

THE VICTIMS

Outcasts from society, these children's only hope is an education.

THE ANSWER

In this book, an image of war turns into one of promise the same way an education can change a child's future from despair to hope.

ACTION

The book was distributed at several events to raise awareness and donations for this important cause.

RESULTS

The foundation grew 200% in 2010/2011 — meaning more Rwandan children were be able to attend school and have their uniforms, shoes, books, school materials and transportation paid for. Foundation Rwanda was able to increase their financial support from 150 children to over 510.

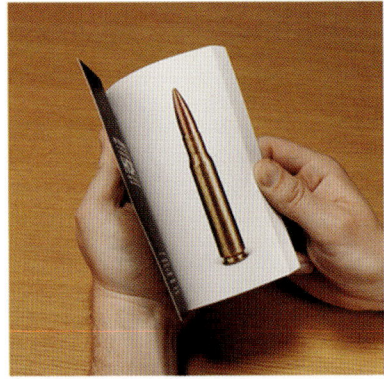

THAT'S A HUGE CHANGE FOR THE BETTER

CREATED BY JWT SOUTH

We're a dynamically structured unit of JWT, 300+ people strong, based in Atlanta with offices in Dallas and Houston. Along with strategic and creative development, we also provide integrated engagement services including digital strategy, social media, media planning and buying, UX, website design/development, search and analytics — all under a single leadership team.

Studio _
Hatch Design
Country _
USA

TARGET MICHAEL GRAVES

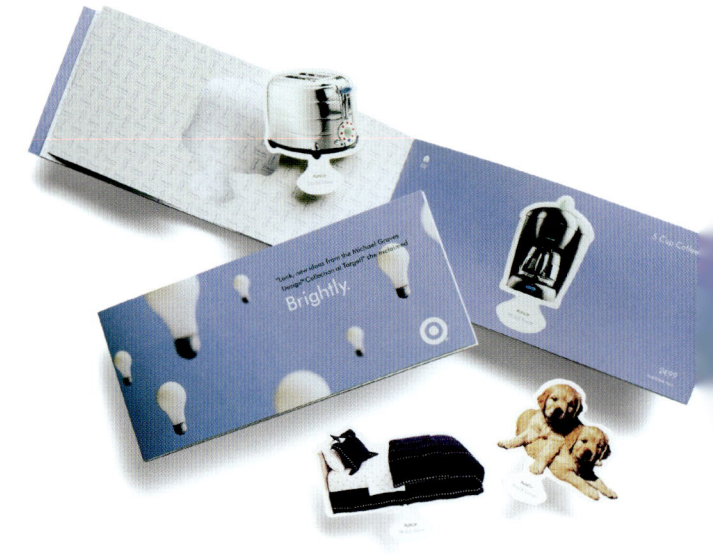

CATALOGUE, BROCHURE, LEAFLET

Client _
Telecom comany TEL
Art Director _
Alekseev Yura
Designer _
Pitertsev Mikhail
Country _
Russia

TEL

Tel is a telecom comany. It is the owner of fibre optic net that covers Moscow and the surrounding region region.

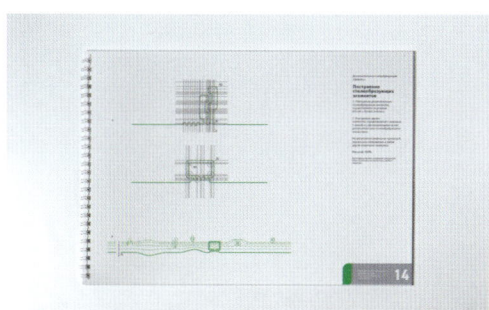
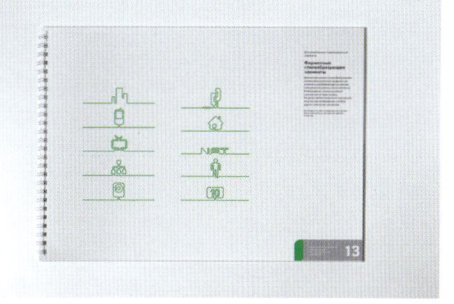

Client _
**Youth Service Kranj
(Mladinski servis Kranj)**
Studio _
Tomato Košir s. p.
Designer _
Tomato Košir
Photographer _
Peter Koštrun
Print _
Grafex
Country _
Slovenia

CONTEMPORARY SLOVENIAN HUMANISTS & SOCIAL SCIENTISTS

This booklet presenting contemporary Slovenian writers was originally created as a give-away promotion at the Frankfurt book fair. The first half presents Slovenian Humanists and the second half Social scientists. It had to be big, eye-catching, and at the same time small enough to fit in a handbag. Our double binding solved the problem.

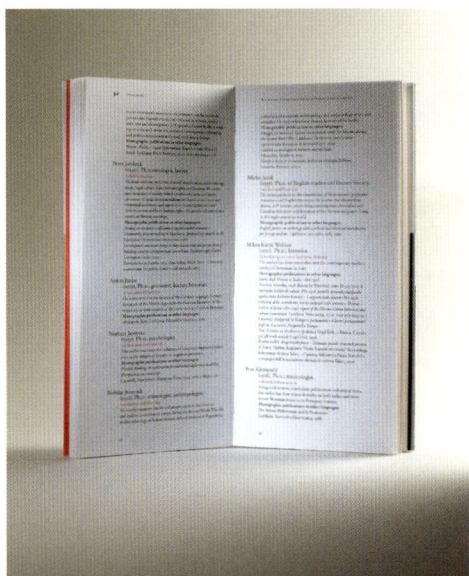
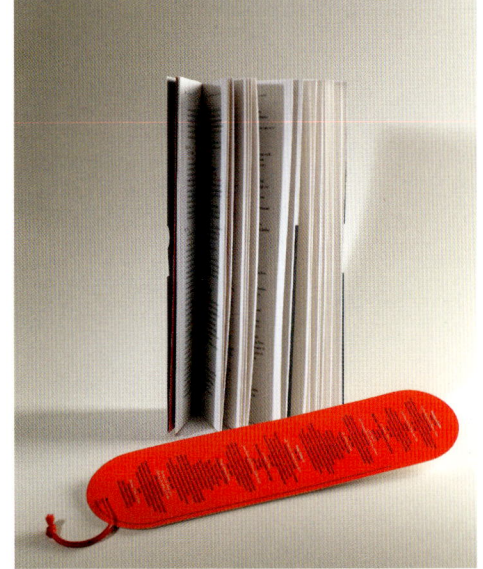

Client _
WAKE FOREST
Agency _
Wildfire Idea
Creative Director _
Mike Grice
Art Directors _
Shane Cranford, Ross Clodfelter
Designers _
Shane Cranford, Ross Clodfelter
Country _
USA

WAKE FOREST UNIVERSITY FOOTBALL

The most successful quarterback in the history of Wake Forest University football recently graduated. Instead of featuring an unproven lineup in the university's marketing materials, Wildfire and Wake Forest Athletics created a fan-focused campaign. Modelled after a football playbook, this Fan Playbook captures the game day experience with an introductory locker room speech, the WFU fight song, a game of matching players to their numbers and WFU eye-black tattoos and a paper football. The weathered, textural design and language was inspired by the no-nonsense, old school coaching style of WFU head football coach Jim Grobe. Other pieces in the campaign include player schedule cards, a senior schedule poster, billboards, an e-blast, tickets, credentials, TV and print.

  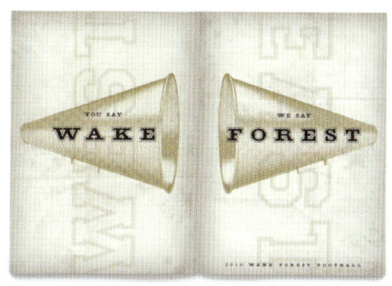
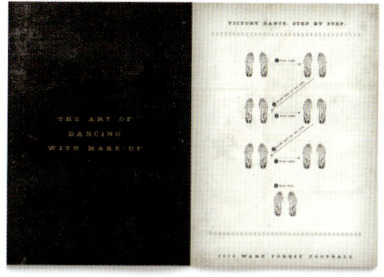 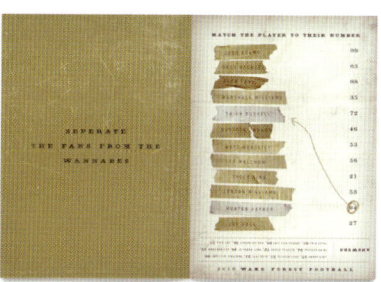 

CATALOGUE, BROCHURE, LEAFLET

Client _
Wall & Decò
Studio _
D+
Designer _
Wladimiro Bendandi
Country _
Italy

WALL & DECÒ

Pocket-sized catalogue dedicated to the great distribution and a collection sample dedicated to large stores and designers for a wallpaper company.

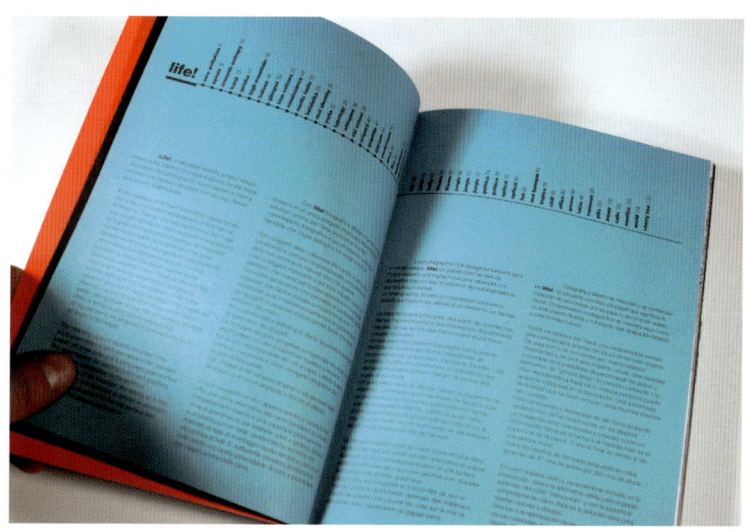

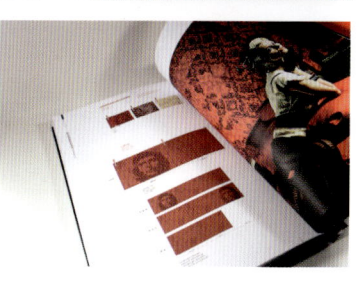

Client _
Torremat
Studio _
Zoo Studio
Creative Director _
Gerard Calm
Designer _
Xavier Castells
Photographer _
Ivan Raga
Country _
Spain

TORREMAT CATALOGUE

Catalogue of a hardware products company.

DIRECT MAIL

Agency _
Alpha245 / Leo Burnett
Creative Directors _
Tan Kien Eng, Theresa Tsang
Art Directors _
Theresa Tsang, Koh Siok Yee
Copyrighters _
Joanne Ng, Lee Pei Sien, Tan Joke Min
Designer _
Koh Siok Yee
Production _
Shara Goh, Ong Chee Hin
General Manager _
Terence Ooi
Country _
Malaysia

A BIGGER HARVEST

To develop an appealing and attention-grabbing communication piece to wish potential and existing clients of Alpha 245 a very happy and prosperous lunar new year, the key objective is to encourage enquiries and generate business opportunities from potential and existing clients.

Mandarin oranges have traditionally been used as gifts to convey wishes of prosperity as orange is pronounced gold in Chinese. Since 2011 was the Year of the Rabbit, we decided to give this gift-giving tradition a little twist. We packed the mandarin oranges, small and big to signify different golden opportunities and shaped them to look like carrots. However, these "carrots" are much larger than real ones and a message that promotes partnership for cultivating a bigger harvest was tagged together. They were given to potential and existing clients to wish them a successful and profitable Year of the Rabbit.

From a list of 18 prospective clients, this communication piece managed to open the doors to 5 new business meetings within the same week that the gift sets were sent. One client even referred two new businesses to the Agency while another client requested the Agency to produce the "carrots" as Chinese New Year premiums for its company. All other existing clients who received the greeting pack contacted the Agency and provided exceptionally encouraging and positive feedback.

Client _
Amena
Creative Director _
Raúl Cepi
Art Director _
David Guillermo López
Copywriter _
Raúl Cepi
Country _
Spain

AMENA DISCOTHEQUE

Amena was a mobile network operator in Spain. We developed an incentive marketing plan "Amena Discotheque", for the commercial area, with a welcome pack. It was represented by a music cabin into a discotheque, where every sales representative is a DISC JOCKEY with the aptitude to control the skills for his sales.

Client _
DEAG Music GmbH
Studio _
Hort
Country _
Germany

AN ORANGE THAT TOOK ON A NEW LIFE

The task was to design a Chinese New Year card to send along with a basket of mandarin oranges to all LB and Arc clients. However, most clients typically receive cards and oranges from other agencies, suppliers and business partners. So the aim was to cut through the clutter by using creativity to change human behaviour.

Throughout the ages, mandarin oranges are normally included in the tradition of gift-giving among the Chinese to convey wishes of prosperity during the New Year. But due to its common presence, no one gives a second thought to its symbolism. So, we decided to change people's perception of the orange as just a fruit. We gave the orange a new lease of life by transforming it into the Chinese zodiac animals for 2010 & 2011 – the Tiger and the Rabbit. We designed a Chinese New Year greeting card containing a special set of stickers bearing an assortment of eyes, nose, ears, etc. that could be used to decorate the oranges so that they resemble a Tiger and a Rabbit. This way, our clients could have fun turning oranges into tigers and rabbits before handing them out to family and friends. The card also doubles up as a backdrop of various sceneries for the orange tigers and rabbits should the recipient decide to take pictures of them and post them online.

We received lots of compliments with requests for additional stickers (which we had to reprint due to the unexpected demand). Many clients used the orange tigers and rabbits as home decor, snapped pictures of them in front of various backgrounds and sent them out as e-cards from our mini site. Many even uploaded them onto Facebook and kept them as profile pictures throughout Chinese New Year.

Due to its popularity and demand, we are expanding the stickers into a series of the other animals in the Chinese zodiac – Dragon, Snake, Horse, Goat, Monkey, Rooster, Dog, Pig, Rat and Ox – which will not only be given to clients, but also sold commercially to the public in gift stores and malls. We have since coined a name for this series heralding the Tiger as the pioneer – Harry Meow (as in Harimau – the Malay translation for tiger) & Friends.

DIRECT MAIL | 151

Client _
Klein Bier
Agency _
Beats
Creative Director _
Sulivan Cruz
Art Directors _
Edson Vaz, Ronaldo Shimizu
Copywrighter _
Sulivan Cruz
Designer _
Ronaldo Shimizu
Photographer _
Ronaldo Shimizu
Country _
Brazil

THE BEER THAT CAME AT THE RIGHT TIME

For the release of the new Klein Bier ESP Pale Ale, a British origin beer, Beats created a Direct Marketing inspired by the icon of British punctuality, Big Ben.

Client _
Adris group
Agency _
Bruketa & Zinic OM
Creative Director _
Davor Bruketa, Nikola Zinic, Miran Tomicic
Art Directors _
Nebojsa Cvetkovic
Copywrighter _
Ivan Cadez
Designer/Illustrator _
Nebojsa Cvetkovic
Photographer _
Domagoj Kunic, Biljana Knebl
Origami Designe _
Sanja Srbljinovic Cucek
Account Executive _
Martina Ivkic
Production Manager _
Vesna Durasin
DTP _
Marko Ostrez
Country _
Croatia

ORIGAMI INVITATION

A prestigious regatta Adris RC44 Cup was held in Rovinj for the first time, bringing together the biggest names from the world of sailing. The host of the regatta was Hotel Lone, a unique hotel, a place of inspiration and a sort of a showcase of Croatia's creative industry. Therefore, the invitation sent to the guests integrates the sailing motif with the inspirational, artistic nature of Hotel Lone – it is a box containing an invitation and a unique example of an origami sailing boat made in Lone colour and a stylised wave motif, that was designed especially for this occasion by Sanja Srbljinovic Cucek, a renowned origami art promoter in Croatia.

DIRECT MAIL

Client _
Erste & Steiermärkische Bank
Studio _
Bunch
Creative Director _
Denis Kovač
Country _
Croatia

ERSTE BANK

Below the line collateral for Croatia's leading bank. We have worked closely with
Erste Bank to refresh the existing direct mail communication channel on some of their
brands including Diners and Visa.
The response to the direcct mail campaign exceeded all expectations.

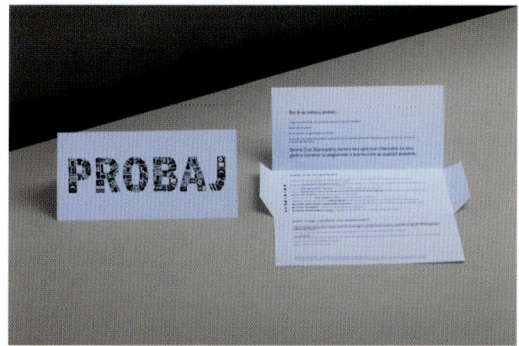

Client _
Aguirre Newman
Creative Director _
Cristina Rodriguez
Art Director _
David Guillermo López
Copywriter _
Daniel Gómez
Country _
Spain

BIGGER IS POSSIBLE

Aguirre Newman is a Spanish construction company. This direct mail was developed with the concept "bigger is possible". The objective is to report to logistic sector that Aguirre Newman has all the space that they require. This concept was represented with a mailing of four envelopes and letters. They started by reading a letter in A4 and ending with a letter of 1 metre.

Client _
Mercedes-Benz
Agency _
Drehmoment Agentur für kreatives Marketing
Art Director _
Eugen Trubatschow
Copywriter _
Christoph Rieckmann
Designers _
Tim Glashoff, Melanie Gabriel
Country _
Germany

FAST AND EASY

A mailing that demonstrates the promptness and simplicity of the Mercedes-Benz windshield repair services while opening it.
Just open the envelope and pull out the glass damage.

1.

2.
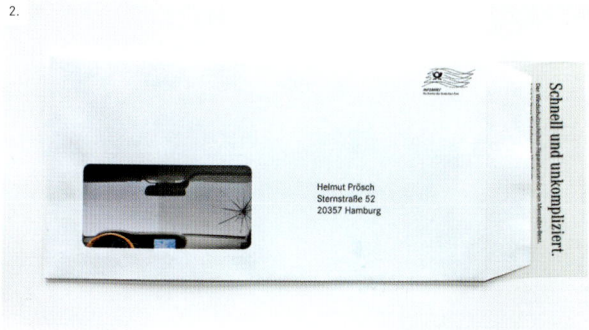

3.

Client _
Harley-Davidson Numero Uno Milan
Agency _
Grey Milan
Creative Director _
Francesco Emiliani
Art Director _
Gaetano Cerrato
Copywriter _
Francesca Andriani
Photographer _
Giovanni Santarelli D'angelo
Head of Art _
Francesco Fallisi
Country _
Italy

HARLEY-DAVIDSON HANDLEBARS 2011 CALENDAR

Thanks to Harley-Davidson Numero Uno Milan, 2011 will be my year as a protagonist. It's now time for me to personally experience what it means to be in a place where I'll never be alone, where I'll be the centre of attention. This is a special place, a place that can trigger thrilling emotions: amazement, respect, desire, inspire admiration and thousands of other unthinkable feelings. Month by month I'm going to realise I don't want to be anywhere else. Thanks to this calendar, I'll put my hands on these handlebars and I'll ride my motorbike for 365 days.
Follow me; it'll be the best trip ever. My trip.

Client _
Elmsta 3000 Horror Fest
Agency _
Saatchi & Saatchi Stockholm
Art Directors _
Gustav Egerstedt, Afshin Moeini and Mårten Hedbom
Photographer _
Alexander Crispin
Client _
Roger Glassel Account manager, Eva Håkansson
Country _
Sweden

COMFORT PILLOW

An invitation to promote a Swedish horror film festival. This exclusive pillow was sent to the members of the festival. On the tag time and date of the festival was printed. The idea was to create something that could live longer than a regular invitation.

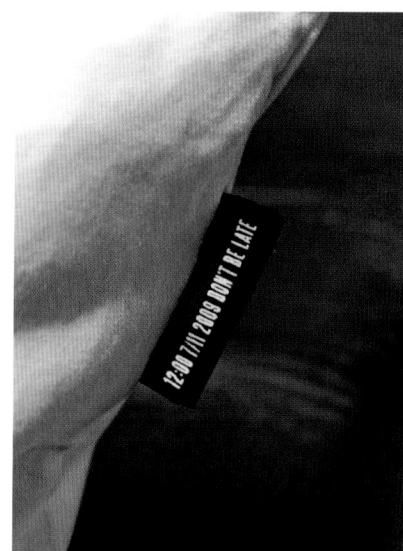

Client _
Ikea
Agency _
Memac Ogilvy
Creative Director _
Ramzi Moutran
Art Director _
Leo Rosa Borges
Copywriter _
Ali Mokdad
Designer _
Leo Rosa Borges
Country _
United Arab Emirates

IKEA FLAT PACK DIRECT MAILER

Ikea wanted to get consumers excited about their latest range of bedroom furniture and accessories. The stylish new furniture needed to stand out.
To supplement the Ikea catalogue, a special targeted piece of communication was created. We designed a pop-up mailer, which looked like an Ikea flat pack box. When opened, a brand new bedroom popped up before their eyes.

DIRECT MAIL

Client _
Percos Laboratories
Agency _
RAPP
Creative Director _
Yesid Suarez
Art Director _
Yesid Suarez
Copywriter _
Pablo Castro
Designer _
Carolina Ramirez
Photographer _
Sergio Tapia
Collaborator _
Carlos Jaramillo
Country _
Colombia

A FAT MAILING FOR DERMASOLUTIONS

It was DM piece, which contained information about a new and amazing product at the time: patches that reduce fat on localised body parts. What was great about this piece is that, it explained the benefit of patches by just opening the DM. It was impossible to open the mail piece without eliminating the fat on the waist. Simple, but great.
The message is: When there's excess, get rid of it.

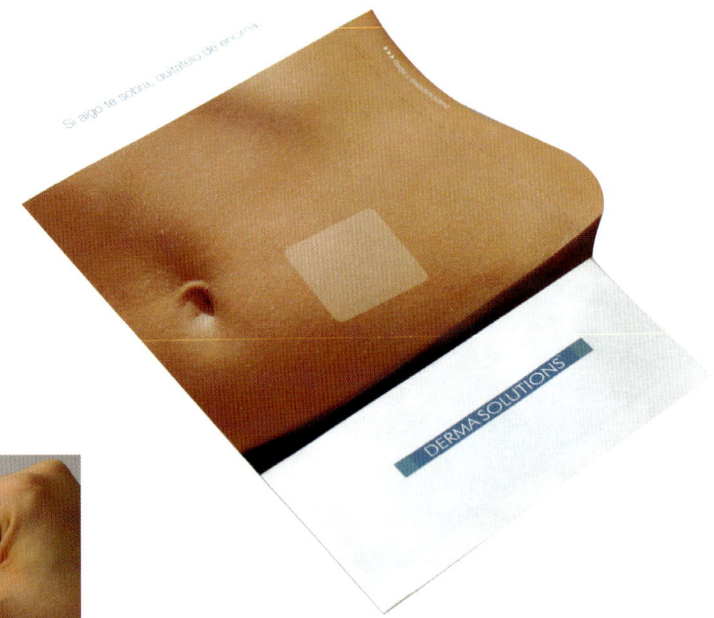

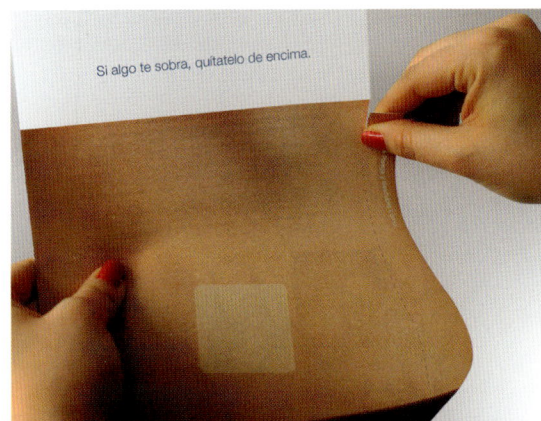

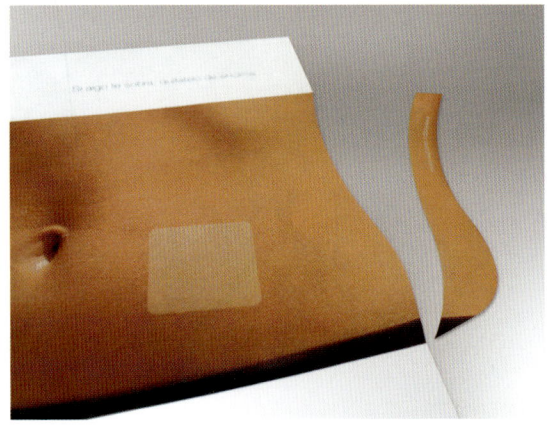

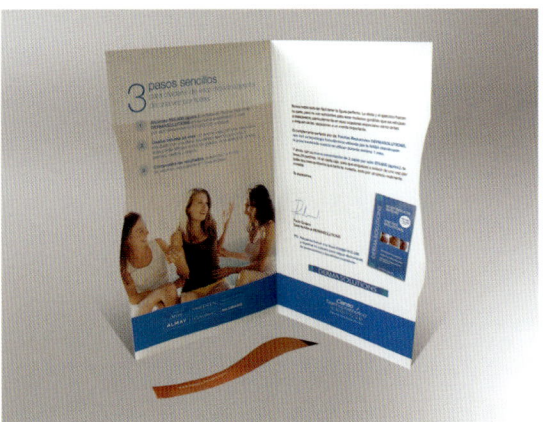

Client _
BMW Ibérica
Creative Director _
Raúl Cepi
Art Director _
David Guillermo López
Copywriter _
Raúl Cepi
Country _
Spain

EQUIPADOS

BMW is a German automobile motorcycle and engine manufacturing company. Equipados is an incentive marketing plan which encourages the chiefs of services and refill, to work together. Inspiring them to be the best team and win a final prize.
The concept was represented graphically by a pencil with just two tips.

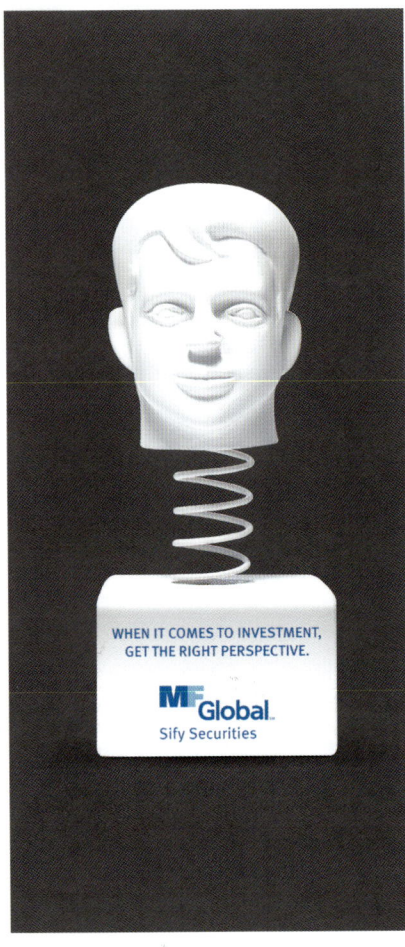
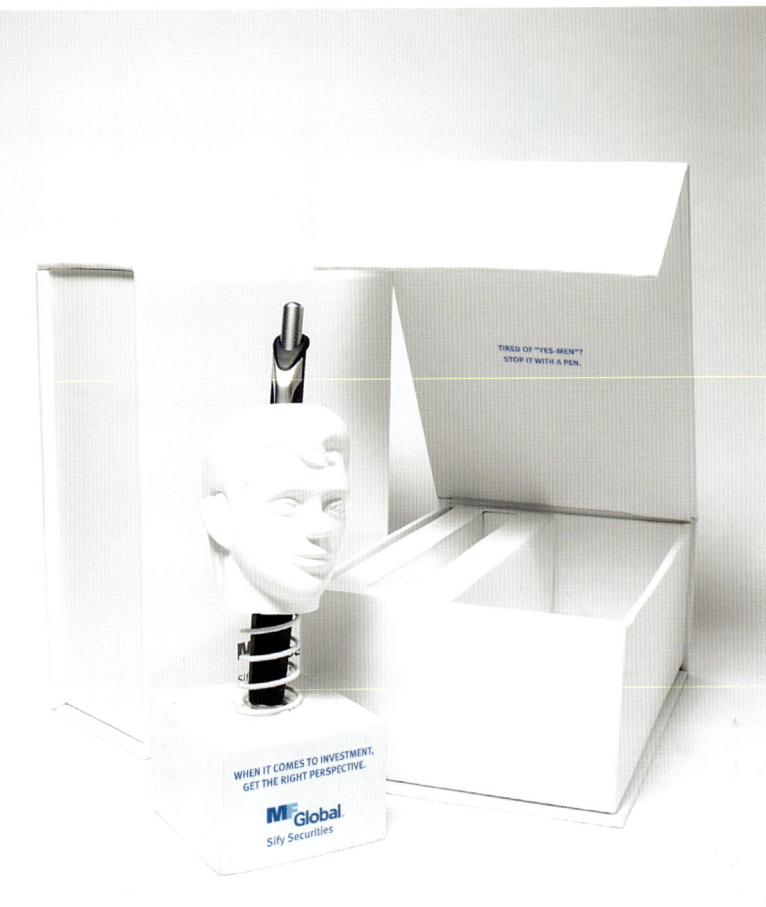

STOP THE NODDING

When MF Global, one of the world's largest brokerage and research houses conducted a dipstick in the market, it was revealed that investors were looking for 3 key things from their broking firm – wealth creation, knowledge and an honest opinion. It also revealed that high-net-worth individuals (HNIs), whose primary TG were always surrounded by Yes Men when it came to investments and how MF Global made for a trusted partner in those scenarios.

Banking on the insight of honest opinion, we crafted a 3600 campaign for MF Global – "Get the right perspective", which positioned the brand as a trusted ally to investors. This Direct Mailer is an extension of the thought and was integral in making the entire campaign a huge success.

The idea of the Nodder was inspired from our toddling days. Back then we often had toys that aped the wobbling head-nod used to express yes. The Direct Mailer was built on this premise as a pen holder and was also the visual symbol for our TVC. Each time you placed a pen in it, the nodding would stop, thus emphasising our thought of saying No to Yes Men.

The DM was sent to 500 current and potential customers of MF Global as a reminder to our TVC. The response was astounding. Appreciation came in from all corners. MF Global received a large number of emails and phone calls praising the Direct Mailer. Recipients adorned their desks and workstations with it. The buzz resulted in hot leads and made MF Global a preferred investment partner to investors from across India.

Client _
MF Global Sify Securities Pvt. Ltd.
Agency _
Six Inches Communication Pvt. Ltd.
Creative Directors _
Pravin Shah, Sanjay S
Art Director _
Reshma Basankar
Copywriter _
Amit Badle
Designer _
Souchitra Sarkar, Sachin Rane
Photographer _
Domagoj Kunic, Biljana Knebl
Origami Designer _
Sanja Srbljinovic Cucek
Account Executive _
Martina Ivkic
Production Manager _
Vesna Durasin
DTP _
Marko Ostrez
Country _
India

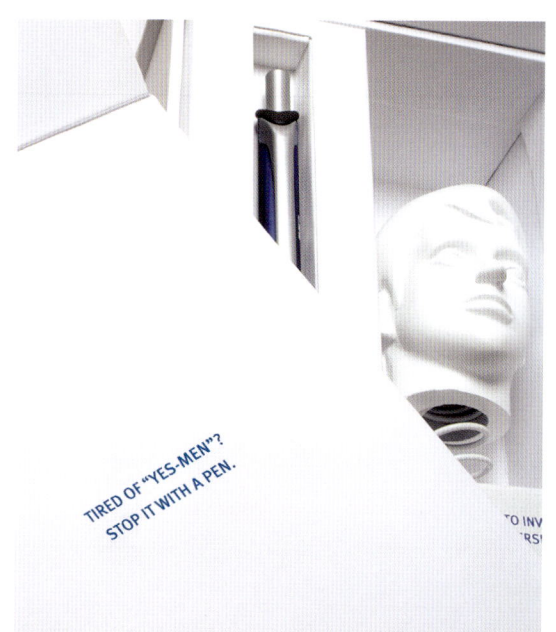

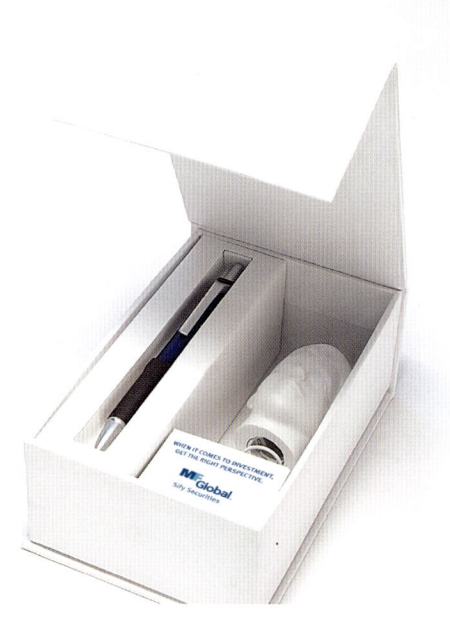
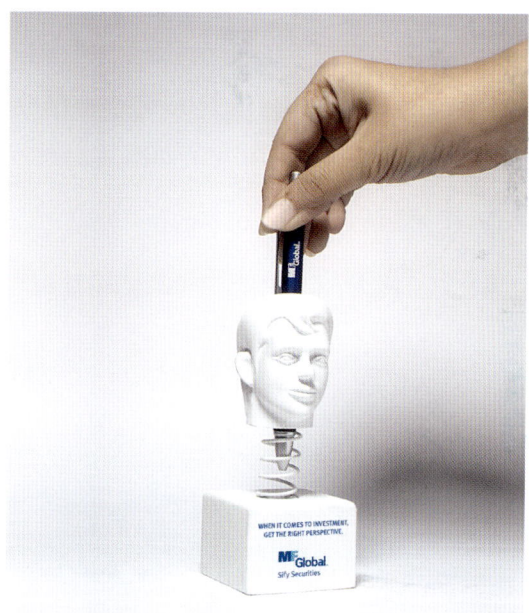

JAMES NEWMAN

James asked us to create a promotional piece and a new folio book of his latest work that could be sent to agencies.

An A5 booklet was developed, along with an A3 poster which folded to an envelope format to house the booklet. By doing this we were able to showcase hero images in a poster format, which are revealed as the recipient opens the package. There were four poster variations created that would be relevant to different agencies.

The A5 booklets have a smaller A6 cover. These smaller covers added a nice look while also providing a practical space for the text details, leaving the A5 booklet free to display the imagery. There were four different stock colours used for the A6 covers.

The folio book was created in the same A3 format that we have previously done for James. The book was given a small design update so it sits in line with the booklets and posters.

Client _
James Newman
Studio _
Takt Studio
Creative Director _
Tait Oosthuizen
Country _
Australia

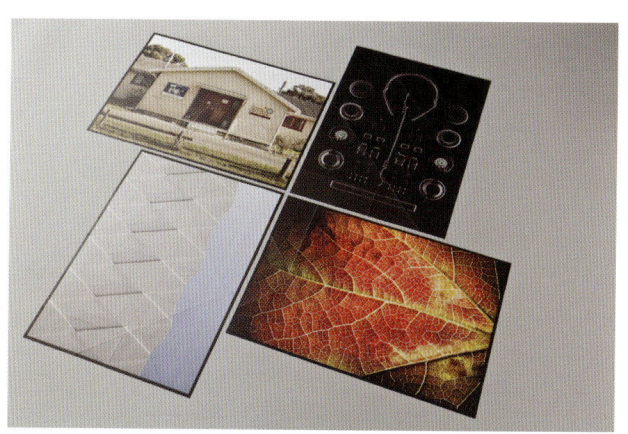

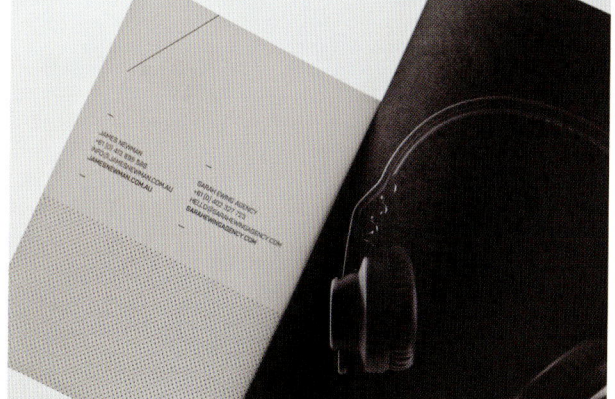

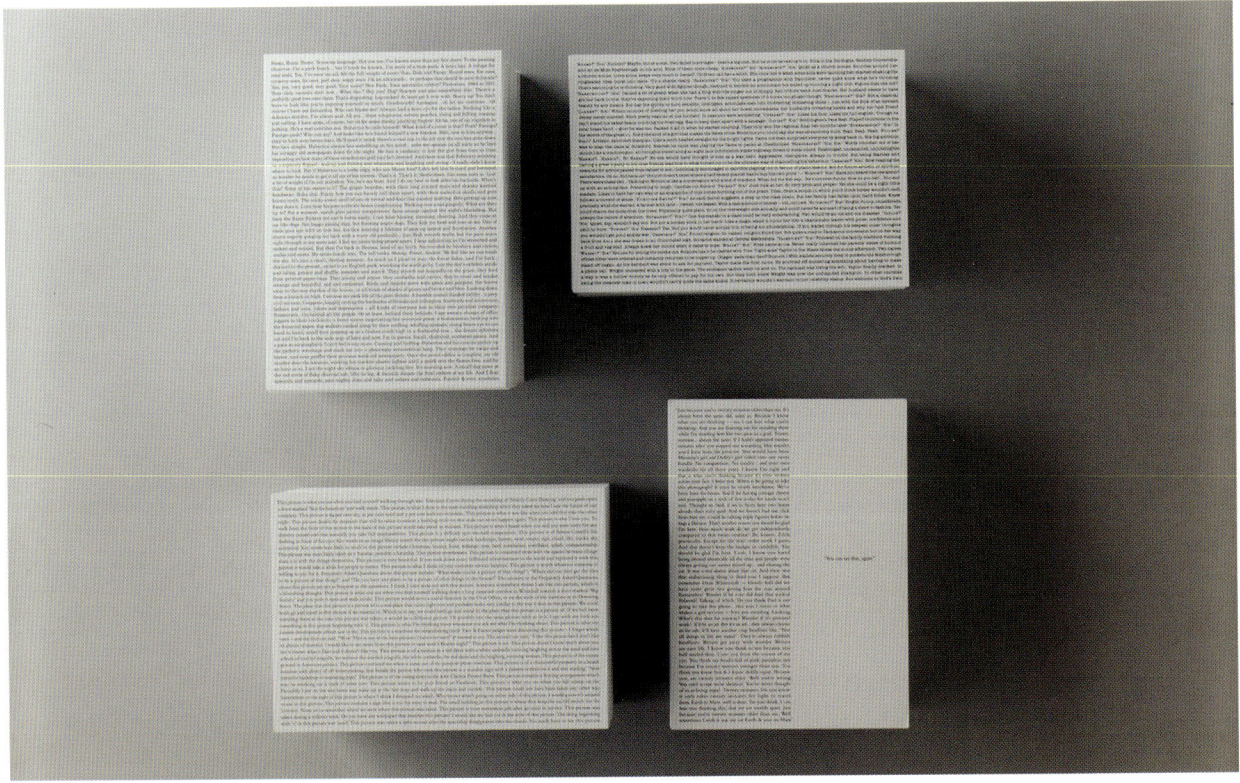

A PICTURE SPEAKS A THOUSAND WORDS

Paul Thompson, a London based photographer asked us to consider designing a second DM campaign following the success of our last campaign with him.
Tired of receiving endless direct mail pieces from photographers featuring Mexican gypsies that they've shot on their travels, we thought it was time for a change.
Our approach was to focus on the personality of the photographer rather than his work. After all most photographers we come into contact with are very capable of taking good shots. What really makes the difference in their selection is probably them, the relationship between art director, client and photographer is key.
We developed an idea which wouldn't feature photographs at all, just a beautiful and engaging description of them, which was exactly 1000 words. This would hopefully encourage the recipient to go to his website and discover which picture it described. Each description is set out to exactly the same proportions of the picture and uses a typeface which mirrors the subject.

Client _
Paul Thompson
Studio _
The Chase
Creative Directors _
Peter Richardson, Ben Casey
Copywriters _
Ben Casey, Lionel Hatch, Nick Asbury, Jim Davies
Typographers _
Lionel Hatch, Harry Heptonstall
Country _
UK

NAME CARD

Client _
The University Veterinary Hospital at Beit Dagan, Israel
Agency _
Baumann Ber Rivnay / Saatchi & Saatchi
Chief Creative Officer _
Yoram Levi
Creative Director _
Nadav Pressman
Art Directors _
Uri Dagan, Eyal Segal
Copywriter _
Eran (Shushu) Spanier
Designers _
Inbal Nezer, Zehava Gonen-Greenberg
Country _
Israel

ANIMAL X-RAY BUSINESS CARDS

The University Veterinary Hospital at Beit Dagan Israel is known for its expert veterinarians in various fields.
Using the hospital's stock of animal x-ray footage, we created business cards which look like miniature x-ray sheets.
Each doctor had their own animal based on their specialty or preference.

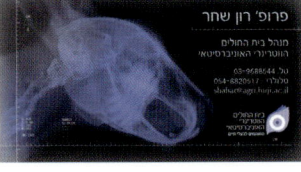
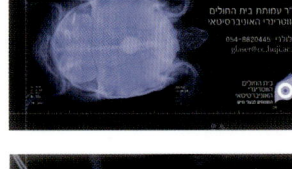

CAROLINE BOISVERT

The client brief was simple. She wanted to make a lasting impression on her potential clients, with a premium professional look. She also wanted to capture the imagination with something that could drive people to her website to find out more information about what she can offer them. Her role of coach, being mostly perceived as abstract, made us want to evoke the results a personal coach could bring. When CEOs have this card in hand, it clearly demonstrates to them that their own leadership potential could grow by making a simple step toward coaching — a promise that they would see almost instant results.

Client _
Caroline Boisvert
Agency _
Chez Valois
Creative Director _
Michel Valois
Art Director _
Michel Valois
Designers _
Michel Valois, Louis Beaudoin
Country _
Canada

Client _
Pat & Co, Brand Coach
Agency _
Chez Valois
Country _
Canada

PAT & CO, BRAND COACH

Pat & Co. is a consultancy firm, specialising in inspirational branding, brand strategy, public speaking, training, coaching, etc. The concept of the card is to use the idea of "revealing what's inside" as a central element, with a series of inspirational stickers placed inside the business cards. When given to someone, that person can easily convey what Pat & Co. can offer — to make brands bloom from the inside with inspirational branding & coaching.

Toy Car

Going to a store and taking a business card is customary. Now, what you can do with it is varies. Tok & Stok turned their business card in an entertainment.
To allude to their easy to assemble furniture, the brand launched an unprecedented action that converts the business card into a little chair. To do so is very simple: just detach the parts marked and put them together. The back of the card has the logo, while the seat takes the essential information such as address and phone number. The action is signed by DDB Brasil.

Client _
Tok & Stok
Agency _
DDB Brasil
Creative Director _
Sergio Valente, Marco Versolato, João Mosterio
Art Directors _
Markus Correa
Copywriter _
Gustavo Tasselli
Account Supervisors _
Polika Teixeira, Marcia Aguiar, Suzana Poli and Marcelo Trivelato
Advertiser's Supervisor _
Regis Dubrule, Ghislaine Dubrule and Flávia Lucena
Country _
Brazil

Client _
EBOLAINDUSTRIES
Agency _
ENFANTS TERRIBLES / EBOLAINDUSTRIES
Executive Creative Directors _
Mizio Ratti, Riccardo Quartesan
Creative Directors _
Hilija Russo, Marika Mangafà, Roberto Ramaglia
Strategy Director _
Valerio Franco
Art Director _
Andrea Trento
Designer _
Antonella Casimirro
Project Managers _
Laura Giunton, Beatrice Mantero
Country _
Italy

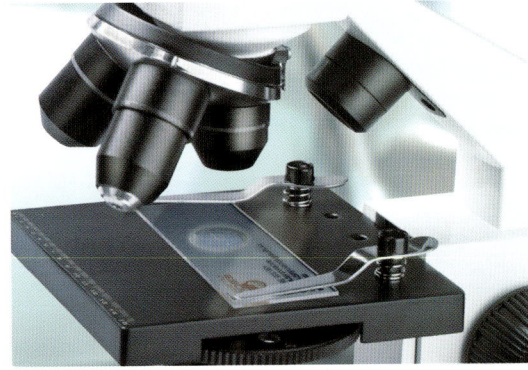

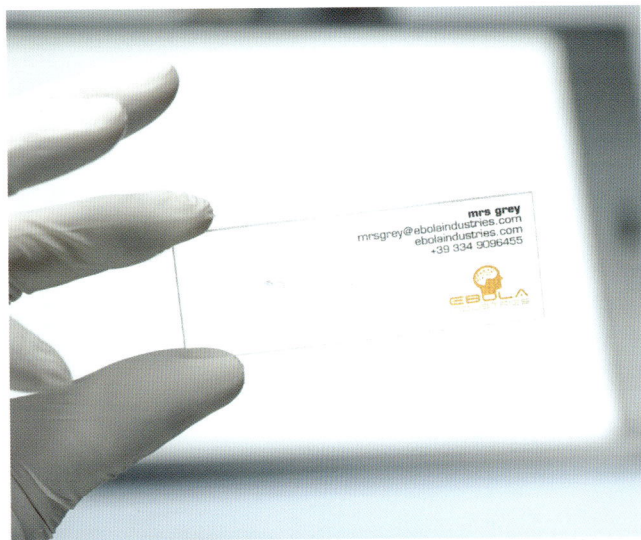

EBOLAINDUSTRIES' IDENTITY

Ebolaindustries was the first Italian viral agency. Since its appearance in the market, back in 2006, ebolaindustries' professionals introduce themselves with a pseudonym: Mr White, Mr Blue, Mr Orange, Mrs Green, Mrs Silver, etc. Over time we felt the need to add an extra boost of impact to our visual presentation in the real world, not just the digital one, by having a business card that would immediately convey the unconventional and viral nature of our approach and business.

That is why the new ebolaindustries business cards emulate the lab slides: in addition to the pseudonym and the image of the Ebola Virus in the reference colour, there are also the real names of the professionals, but they are only visible under a microscope lens.
Cards are made in perspex of 2 millimetres width, with laser-engraved names, font size 0.5mm.

Client _
Ángeles Rubio
Agency _
F33
Photographer _
La Industrial
Country _
Spain

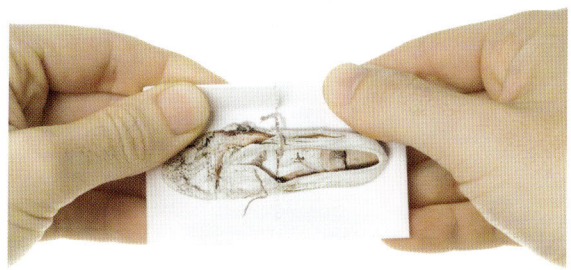

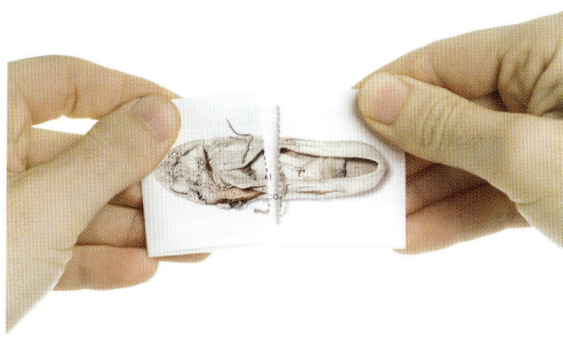

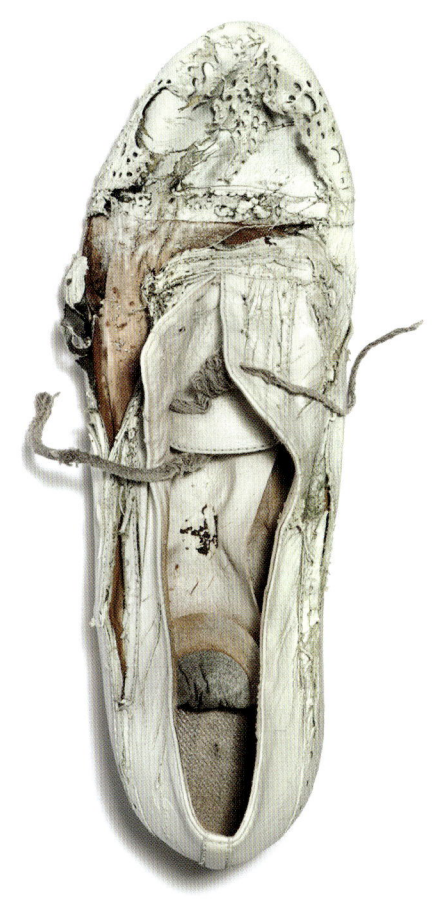

ÁNGELES RUBIO

Identity and stationery items for a shoe designer who intends to get rid of the old and make room for the new.

Client _
Cora Hillebrand
Studio _
Lundgren+Lindqvist
Photographer _
Cora Hillebrand
Country _
Sweden

CORA HILLEBRAND IDENTITY

Our professional relationship with Cora goes back several years and our friendship even further. Apart from documenting our own work, we have involved her in several client projects where keen eye has been a great asset. Lacking a proper business card and a printed portfolio, Cora was in dire need of both promotional material and a cohesive visual presence. Often carrying heavy equipment, Cora wanted something that she could leave behind to clients that would not require an extra visit due to its sheer size. The solution was a combined business card and mini portfolio. We designed a sturdy envelope (using textured Rives Silk stock), in the shape of a Polaroid picture, with an open front. On the envelope, we printed Cora's contact details, much in line with a traditional business card. The insides of the envelopes were printed in bright blue. We selected nine different images from different projects by Cora which were printed on cardboard and perforated for easy detachment. This allows Cora to compose various mini portfolios customised for different client types. We also perforated printer friendly paper for quick updates.

NAME CARD

MURMURE
communication
&design
&art

LE MURMURE

SIMON ROCHÉ
Graphiste Illustrateur
06.15.01.60.11

www.murmure.me
contact@murmure.me

M

MURMURE
communication
&design
&art

LE MURMURE

CYRILLE BAER...
Respons...
06.81...

www.murmure.me

M

MURMURE
communication
&design
&art

rue de la Miséricorde
Caen - France
.73.17.94

www.murmure.me

M

MURMURE
communication
design
&art

...IROL
...istique
.33.54

www.murmure.me

M

MURMURE
communication
&design
&art

LE MURMURE

PAUL RESSENCOURT
Directeur Artistique
06.66.41.01.78

www.murmure.me
contact@murmure.me

M

Agency _
Murmure Agency
Country _
France

CONTACT 2.0

Contact 2.0 shows black cards at first view with a subtle typographic varnished pattern, then when in contact with the hand, the information they contain of each member of the agency appears. On one side is the agency logo, and on the other side, a typographic pattern made from words that characterise the different skills of the agency on a colour background, creating a visual space that can be played with. Through this series, Murmure shows how a playful concept can be transformed into an application for communication. By exploiting this idea, the agency conveys both classical information but also concepts, which characterise specific tastes.

Client _
Franco Caligiuri
Agency _
Rethink Communications
Creative Directors _
Chris Staples, Ian Grais
Copywriter _
Marcus McLaughlin
Designer _
Rory O'Sullivan
Studio Artist _
Justin Renvoize
Account Services _
Jennifer Maloney
Country _
Canada

FINANCIAL ADVISOR BUSINESS CARD

Ideally, you can trust your financial advisor to sell before a downturn and buy stocks before they go up. This is a double-sided business card to communicate this dual promise.

Client _
Norburn Model Aircraft Supply
Agency _
Rethink Communications
Creative Directors _
Ian Grais, Chris Staples
Designer _
Jeff Harrison
Print Producer _
Sheila Santa Barbara
Studio Artist _
Richard Parkes
Printers _
Prismtech Graphics
Account Services _
Ailsa Brown, Michelle Evers
Country _
Canada

NORBURN MODEL AIRCRAFT SUPPLY BUSINESS CARD

This unique business card for Norburn Model Aircraft Supply was created by printing and laser die-cutting balsa wood that can be assembled into a small and functional glider.

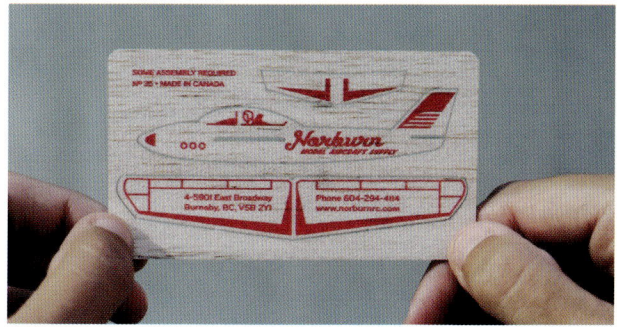

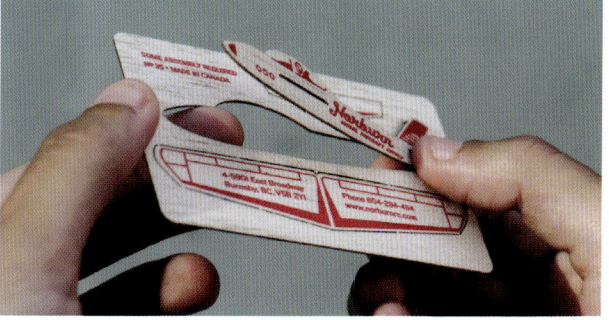

Client _
Aris Nasios
Creative Director _
Sophia Georgopoulou
Designer _
Sophia Georgopoulou
Country _
Greece

ARIS NASIOS BUSINESS CARD

Aris Nasios is a craftsman working in the fields of plasterworks, painting and decorating interiors. He wanted something unique for his business card, showing a handcraft character. As a result, an actual rubber stamp was created that can be used on any material and texture.

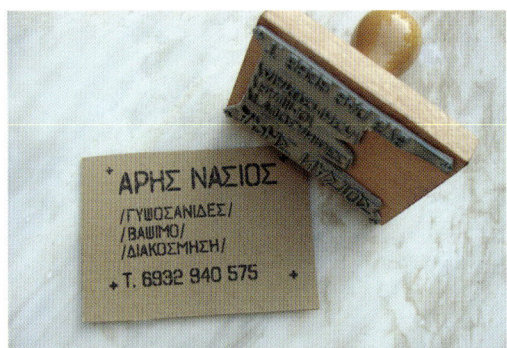

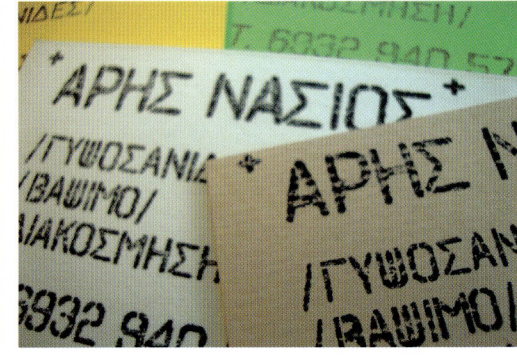
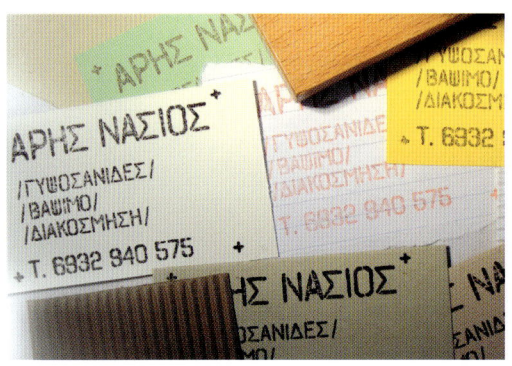

Studio _
Strange Design
Art Director _
Goh Yam Hwee
Country _
Singapore

STRANGE DESIGN NAMECARD

Name card for Strange Design, a design studio in Singapore. The straightforward and bold typographic design is laser cut on a thick black card with no printing needed.

Agency _
Memac Ogilvy
Creative Director _
Ramzi Moutran
Art Director _
Leo Rosa Borges
Copywriter _
James Bisset
Designer _
Leo Rosa Borges
Country _
United Arab Emirates

UNDERSIZED RECESSION BUSINESS CARDS

THE CHALLENGE:

With growing economic concerns and shrinking marketing budgets, we needed to tell clients and prospective clients that indeed, because of the recession, we are more relevant to them now than ever.
What we needed was a simple, cheap and effective way to do this.

SOLUTION:

We created undersized business cards with appealing designs and thought, provoking lines to drive potential clients to www.ogilvyonrecession.com — a website offering smart strategies to deal with the downturn.
Responses were overwhelming. Aside from being an engaging icebreaker with our desired audience, we had produced an insightful, relevant and targeted campaign, by saving rather than spending.

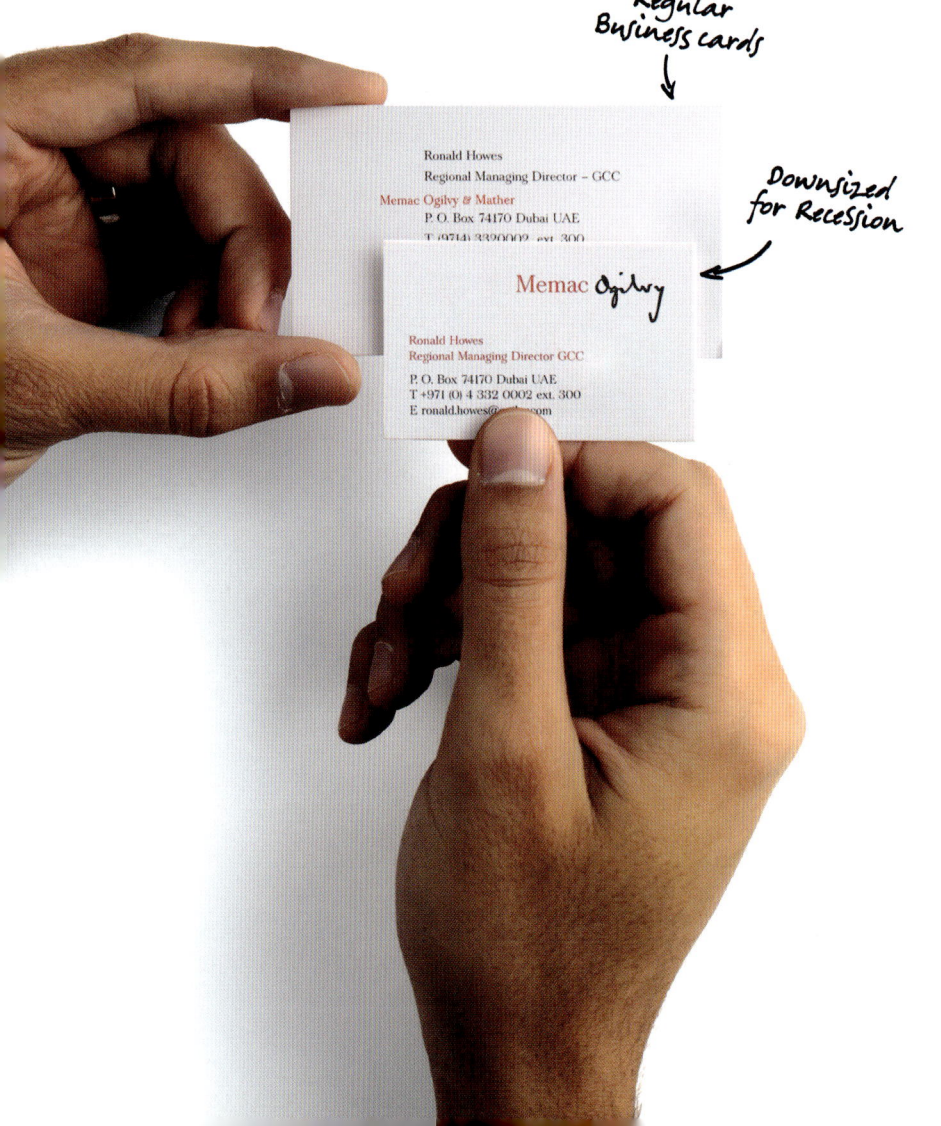

PACKAGE

Client _
East 9th Brewing
Studio _
Bigdog Creative
Creative Director _
Josh Lefers
Copywriter _
Josh Lefers
Art Director _
Kane Marevich
Designer _
Kane Marevich
Country _
Australia

DOSS BLOCKOS BEER

The request from the client was to create a brand that took in all of the values of the squatting culture that had brewed the original beer recipe. We created Doss Blockos as the name after a famous dispute in New York between squatters and developers at Dos Blockos on East Ninth Street. The different elements that made up the brand took their values from street art (we searched and found figures from a wall painting), the international squatting symbol (circle with the bent tick through it) and the bag itself we derived from the history of being allowed to drink in public with brown paper bags. It gave it that final element of street, meets premium, which was also part of the brief, hence appealing across a greater market demographic.

Creative Director _
Tony Ibbotson
Designer _
Andi Yanto
Finishing Artist _
Greg Coles

BUILD YOUR OWN

The aim was to create a unique gift to give our clients at Christmas and to act as a new business introduction. It needed to remind them of who we are and the long hours that we put into our work. It needed to feature all of our staff, reflect our creativity and sense of humour. The print run was 5000 labels.
We obtained high quality cleanskin wines and created our own labels. Each label was based on one staff member. It included a number of facial features and the client is encouraged to BYO — Build Their Own. The wine and the label is the perfect substitute for when the real thing cannot be there.

TANQ

In order to create labels and packaging for the Tanq vodka, to keep the graphics very friendly and have every element of the project reusable while appealing to a large demographic in a way they can relate to, the concept of personality types allowed people to relate to the product on a personal level while having fun. The box is made of recycled cardboard and every part of the game is reusable in one way or another to keep it environmentally friendly. The box opens up into a board game, which can then be played with the bottles acting as characters.

Designer _
Devon Drumm
Country _
Canada

Client _
Sony Computer Entertainment Europe
Agency _
GR/DD
Designer _
Tim Smith
Illustrator _
Tim Smith
Photographers _
Tim Smith, Simon Yuen
Country _
UK

EYEPET

EyePet is Sony's first mainstream Augmented Reality game. Released for the PlayStation 3, the game uses a camera to allow a virtual pet to interact with players and real world objects. In conjunction with this release, GR/DD were tasked with creating a media kit that not only educates the recipient of what AR is, but also entices them into the fun and playful world that the 'EyePet' exists in.
Designed to resemble a pet-carry box, the innovative structural engineering broke new ground with its opening mechanic. The box pops out, surprising the receiver by revealing a cute and cheeky EyePet, with vibrant graphics used to reflect the active and family orientated gameplay. A pet photo album, set of stickers, as well as valuable game parts are all cleverly housed within the kit.
GR/DD's solution is a surprising and memorable marketing tool that went onto win numerous design and packaging awards, generating a significant amount of additional PR and media traction.

Agency _
H-57 srl
Creative Directors _
Matteo Civaschi, Gianmarco Milesi
Art Director _
Matteo Civaschi
Copywriter _
Gianmarco Milesi
Designer _
Matteo Civaschi
Country _
Italy

RE-PACK

Project for the reuse of existing packages.
Everything that has contained something can contain something else and can be useful again. Re-Pack is a way to produce, and therefore pollute, less. The more we recycle, the less we have to dispose of.

Client _
Jimmy's Iced Coffee
Agency _
Interabang
Creative Directors _
Adam Giles, Ian McLean
Illustrator _
Chris Raymond
Country _
UK

JIMMY'S ICED COFFEE

Jimmy's mission is to bring proper off-the-shelf iced coffee to the people of the United Kingdom and beyond. It was launched in Selfridges and Harvey Nichols then rolled out across the UK's supermarkets, shops and festivals.
We injected the packaging with a sense of fun — a strong tone of voice and retro styling using hand crafted typography and a playfulness throughout the identity.

Designer _
Julia Kim
Country _
USA

VERY VERY BRIGHT

This was a personal project—designing a light bulb packaging. I took inspiration from the shape of the compact fluorescent light bulb, as it reminded me of soft—serve ice cream.
This idea spurred a series of light bulb packaging, sticking with the theme of frozen treats.

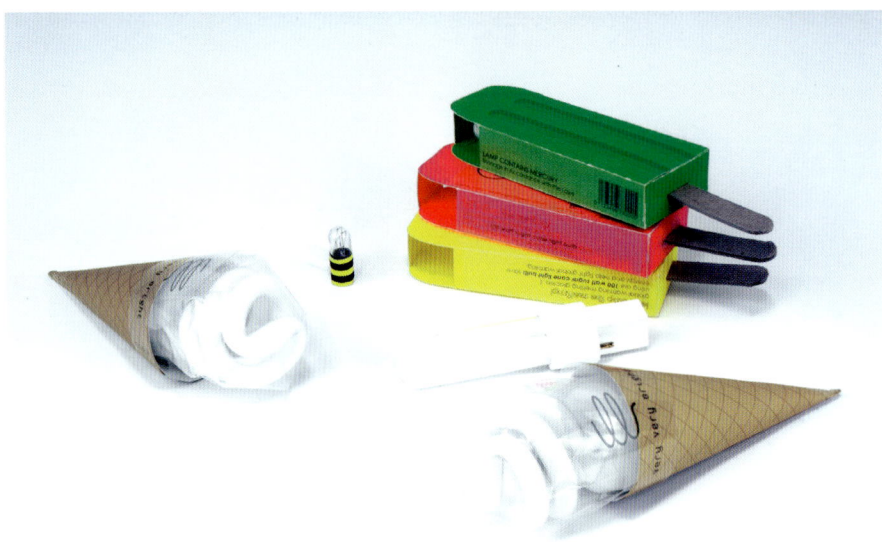

Client _
Escola superior de disseny I Enginyeria de Barcelona

Copywriters _
Martha Robertson, Alfonso Sotelo Nava

Designers _
Martha Robertson, Alfonso Sotelo Nava

Photographer _
Alfonso Sotelo Nava

Render _
Alfonso Sotelo Nava

Country _
Chile

OH MY DOG!

During a workshop of the master of packaging at ELISAVA (Barcelona), we have to design the graphic for a standard line of dog hair care. We start thinking how people wash their dogs, who washes them, when they wash them, etc. We assume that washing the dog is always an adventure. When you try to wash them they run away, or they splash you, or when you finish washing them they run to the mud, or they bite you. So we want to make it easier and funny. In the pack we want to transmit quality, simplicity, fun, and playfulness. We emphasise the context of game and wonder by putting a dog interacting or playing with the logo.

Agency _
Rethink Communications
Creative Directors _
Ian Grais, Chris Staples
Copywriter _
Keri Zierler
Designer _
Jeff Harrison
Photographer _
Clinton Hussey
Studio Artist _
Richard Parkes
Producer _
Ninette Aves
Account Services _
Ailsa Brown, Michelle Evers
Country _
Canada

RETHINK TABLE WINE

This self-promo campaign of table wines showcases Rethink's package design capabilities. The back of each label includes copy crafted to its particular variety of table, giving potential clients a taste of our personality, philosophy and sense of humour.

PROMOTION GIFT AND GOODS

Client _
Houselective
Studio _
Martin Stousland / Anti
Country _
Norway

SOLLI DISKOKLUBB / TREKKFUGL

The title of the album "Trekkfugl" means migrant in Norwegian. "Trekke på et hjørne" refers to prostitutes hanging out on corners trying to get customers. The idea was based around these drugged-up prostitutes.
For the promotion of the release, a cocaine bag was produced, which contained the flyer, stickers and a mirrored paper where you could prepare your "cocaine", which was just baking powder.

Agency _
BFG Communications
Chief Creative Officer _
Scott Seymour
Creative Director _
Amy Songsoonthorn
Art Directors _
Josh Barrett, Adam Sidwell, lex Liebold
Copywriter _
Gregg Hutson
Country _
USA

BFG MIMOBOT FLASH DRIVES

BFG took a gigabyte out of ordinary flash drives by designing a series of "creative monster" flash drives for use as a leave-behind for prospective and current clients. The collaboration with Mimobot® brought three characters to life — Juggerthought, Pixilla and the Messinja, which playfully represent the services BFG provides; our core creative/strategy arm, interactive department and fieldworks branch. The drives always provoke conversation due to their unique blend of form and function, and because of the inherent sharing associated with flash drives, these whimsical characters are a great way to expose BFG's design prowess and fun-loving attitude towards our work to a wide swath of potential clients.

Client _
Barbarela Studio
Agency _
F33
Country _
Spain

PLANT

Promotional item for a firm of exterior architects, which is able to find its habitat in boxes, tables, and gardens of villas.

Client _
Avnet Technology Solutions GmbH/EIZO, Nettetal, Germany
Agency _
BUTTER GmbH, Düsseldorf, Germany
Creative Director _
Nadine Schlichte, Matthias Eickmeyer
Art Directors _
Nadine Schlichte
Copywriter _
Reinhard Henke
Illustratorer _
CGI: Carsten Mainz
Production _
 Lars Schlentzek
Country_
Germany

EIZO Pin-up Calendar

The client briefed us to design a give-away, which advertises an area of expertise of EIZO High-End Monitors: EIZO medical imaging – high precision displays for the examination and diagnosis of radiographs. As you can imagine, the target group (mostly medics) are supposed to be very conservative, so usually get conservative give-aways.
Why not try something new? Not new for craftsmen, who are showered with Pin-up calendars every turn of the year but new for medics – a pin-up calendar. We proposed EIZO to break this taboo and to show the most naked pin-ups ever.

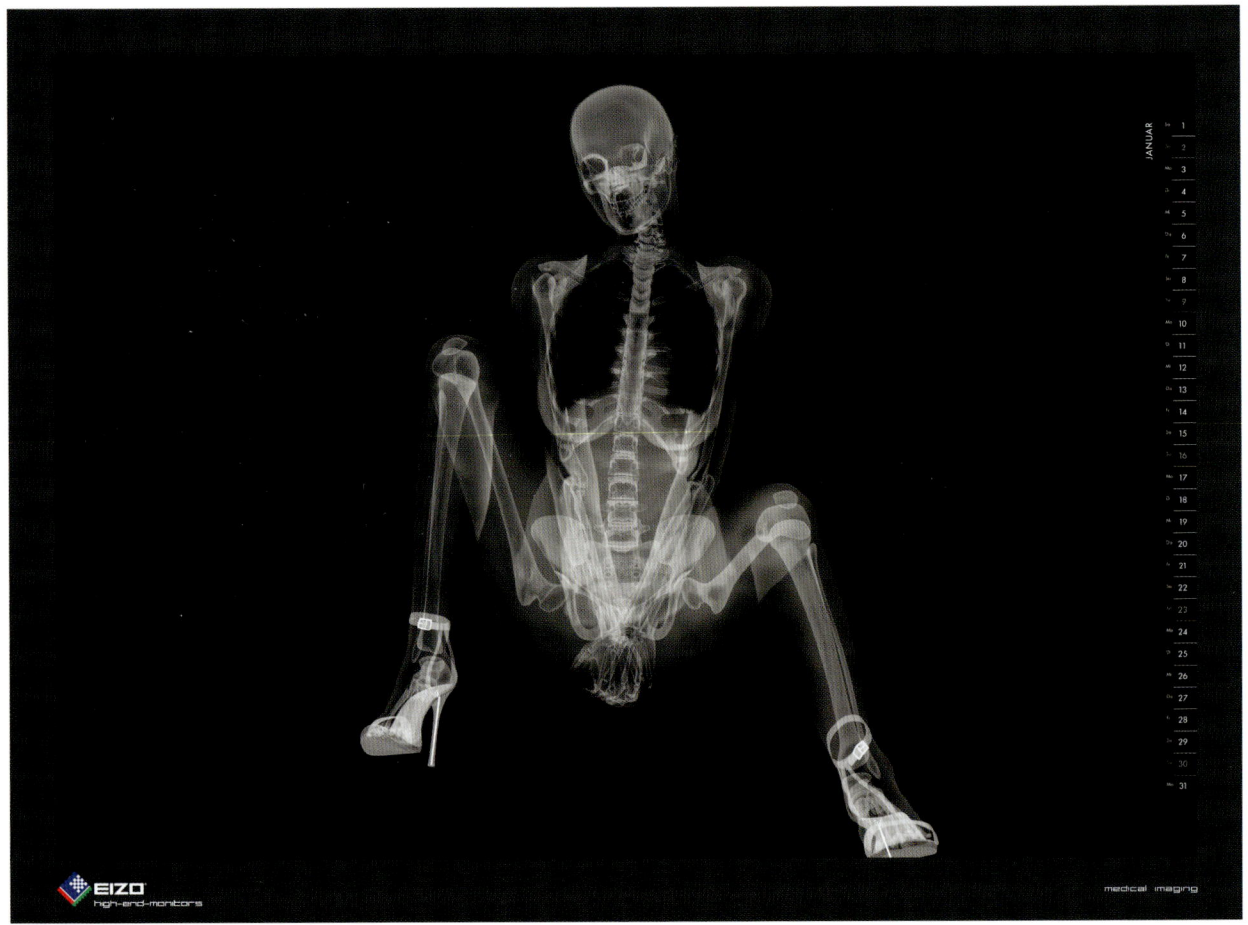

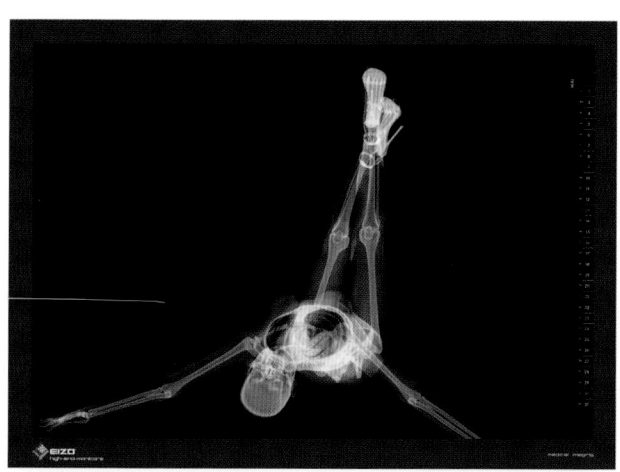
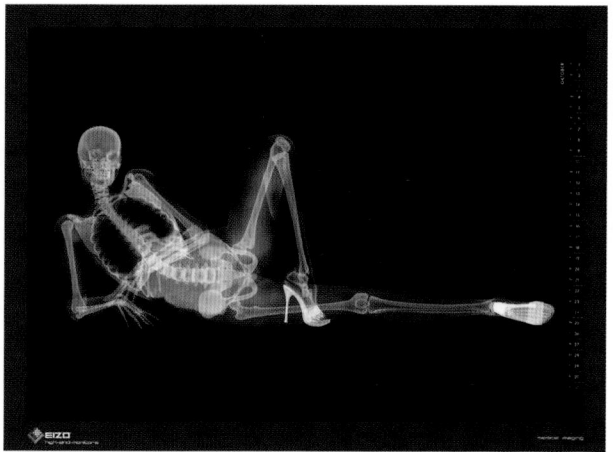
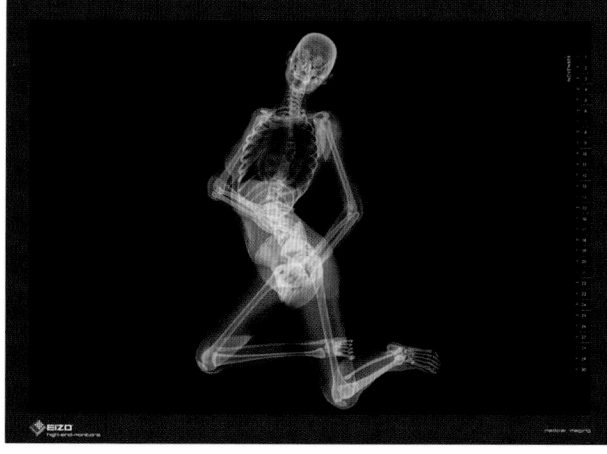
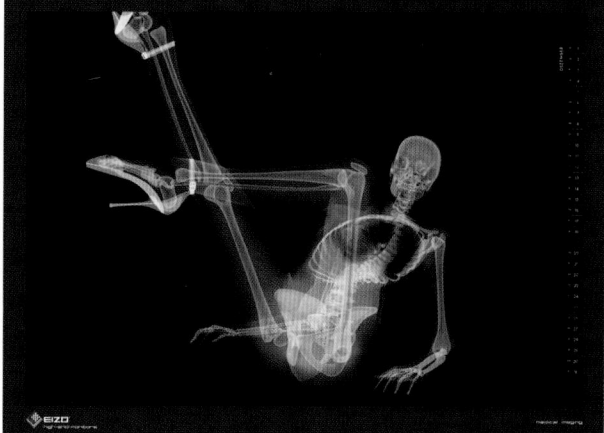

PROMOTION GIFT AND GOODS | 211

Agency _
Cole & Weber United
Creative Director _
Todd Grant
Art Director _
Lance Wei
Copywriter _
Jacob Baas
Designer _
Lance Wei
Country _
USA

HOLIDAY LOG

December is flooded by paper cards celebrating the holidays, many of which end up in the recycle bin. Rather than adding to the clutter with yet another corporate card, we created a holiday experience that would be uniquely Cole & Weber and add value to the recipient's holiday.
What better holiday moment than settling in with a bottle of wine and a warm fire in those cold, long months?
We took logs of fresh pine, milled them to hold a wine bottle and a box of customised matches. Inside the log was a cheerful greeting and instructions on how to properly enjoy the gifts.
Not only did we create a great shipping container for the wine, but that container was the backdrop for a great holiday experience that could last beyond its opening.

Client _
Red Bull Cola
Studio _
Design Friendship
Creative Directors _
Natasha Shah, Chris Hilton
Country _
USA

SAMPLING TOOL

We created and produced an engaging, interactive sampling tool. We sourced, managed and produced this beautifully handmade show case, containing the 17 key/ natural ingredients that make up the Red Bull Cola taste.

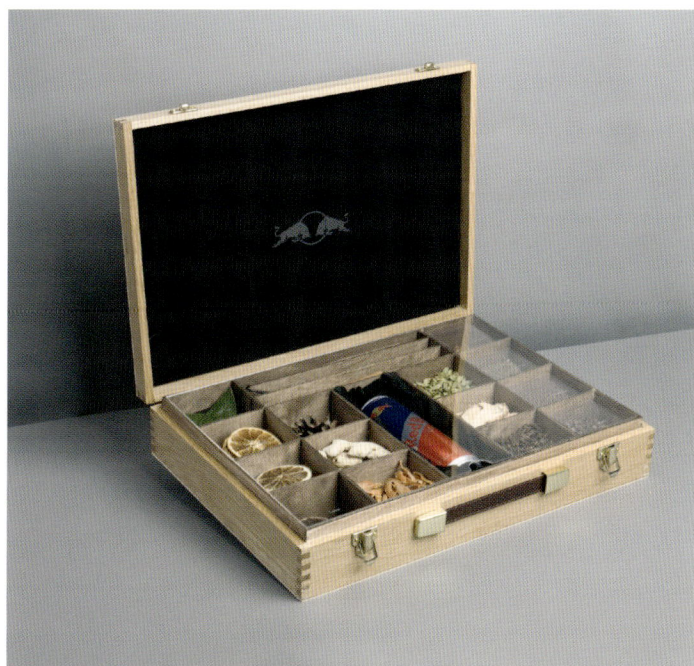

PROMOTION GIFT AND GOODS | 213

Client _
WWF
Agency _
Leo Burnett Colombiana S.A.
Creative Directors _
Germán Espitia, Fernando Hernández, Mauricio Sarmiento
Art Directors _
Fernando Hernandez
Copywriter _
Lukas Calderón
Designer _
Paola Torrenegra
Illustrator _
Wilson González
Photographers _
Oscar Nizo, Germán Rojas
Others/Manufacturers _
Bogota's Botanical Garden (scientific adviser), Rolf Marti , Discerámicos, Smurfit Kappa.
Country _
Colombia

ONE DAILY DROP

This is a commemorative gift for WWF 50th anniversary — the only calendar that lasts for life and generates life.

Thinking how we can save the planet is an idea that circles around our minds every day, which makes us feel a little guilty about what we've done to the world, about our actions and we try to find excuses in others to justify our lack of will to help. If we could just contribute with something small, something not very demanding, that doesn't force us to change our routines, that wouldn't make us environmental activists but simply give us the relief of knowing that we are helping, lightening the weight we carry and making us feel better about ourselves, it would be very comforting.

So, why not? By just moving one finger for three seconds, we can give water to a plant. If we repeat this small act every day, it transforms into an act that helps the planet.

Fill the irrigation pipe with water every month, move your finger 3 seconds every day and you will see a plant growing along the year.

We want that this grain of sand represented by a drop of water to produce life.

Client _
ROLAND SEMPRIE
Studio _
GJP ADVERTISING + DESIGN Toronto
Design Creative Director _
Lisa Greenberg, Trevor Schoenfeld
Designer _
Chris Duchain
Copywriter _
Ross Pryde
Country _
Canada

PERSONAL TRAINER

Roland Semprie is a well-known personal trainer in Toronto, Canada.
Our task was to design a shirt that Roland's clients would be proud to wear in the gym and not just stick in their drawer.

The solution was a t-shirt that gauges how long you have trained with Roland by the amount you sweat. This would be a motivator for Roland's clients, and also let Roland know if they are truly getting a full workout.

The shirt was a complete success for Roland and his clients. They are not only using the shirt during workouts, they are also competing against each other, using the shirt as bragging rights, to see who is working out the most.

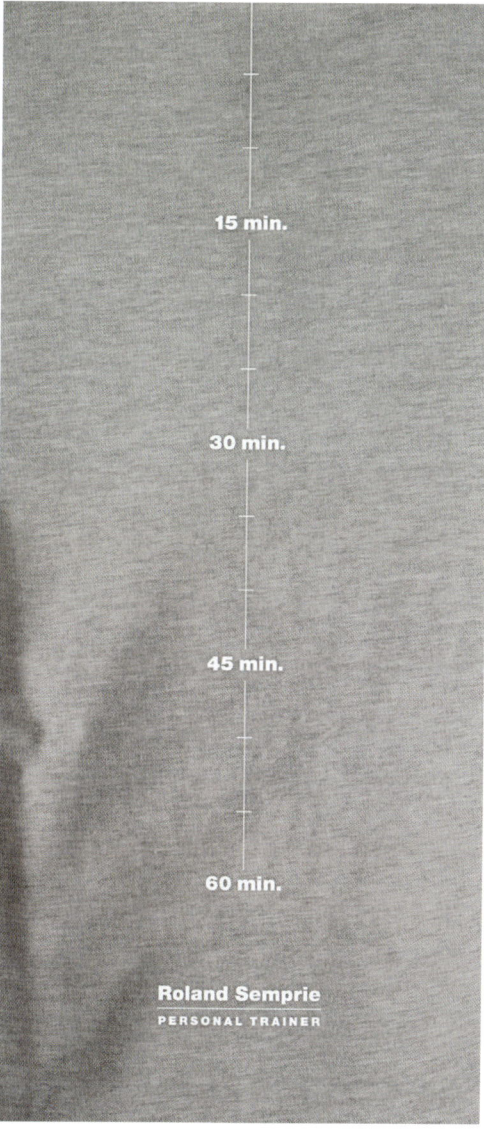
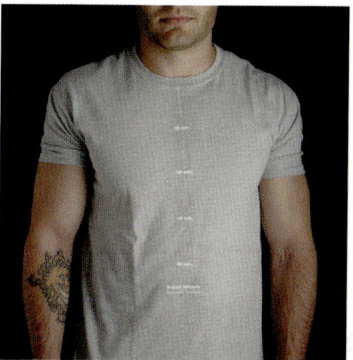

Studio _
Hand Design Studio
Designer _
Vinko Pasalic
Country _
Croatia

HAND DESIGN STUDIO DEVILISH FOOD GIFT BOX

For 8 years now, our studio has been surprising clients with Christmas gifts dubbed "Let's Play With Food". Year after year we try to be original and creative, giving away the best of Croatian hand-made food. This gift dates back to 2008/2009 and its name describes the content to the point. Dalmatian olive oil, Dalmatian almonds and Dalmatian sun-dried chilli peppers are meant to be mixed together and fried in a pan, served hot with a glass of red wine.

Client _
Kerschoffset printing house
Studio _
Hand Design Studio
Creative Director _
Vinko Pasalic
Art Director _
Mirna Saletovic
Designer _
Klaudia Barbic
Photographer _
Igor Sitar
Country _
Croatia

KERSCHOFFSET PROMOTIONAL GIFT — NUANCES MAKE THE DIFFERENCE

In the world of commercial design, timing and deadlines are everything. Being painfully aware of this fact, we have designed a gift that literally tells the story of time & timing in the world of print and design. The gift box consists of a wall clock and the wrist watch that serve as a reminder to designers and agency employees that all prepress materials should be delivered to the printing house on time and that Kerschoffset will deliver all printed materials in time.

An additional element of the gift are little triangles (snippets of time as we like to call them) in various colour — the whole design is based on them. Together with the headline, these little snippets are saying that nuances are important and they actually do make a difference. Nuances of colour and nuances of time in the delivery of printed materials, but the thing that is most important is TIMING.

PANTOGAR MEMO PAD

A specially designed memo pad is made to engage people with the problem of hair loss. As users tear off memo sheets every day, the illustrated person's "hair" becomes thinner and thinner, alerting them of possible hair loss. We then remind them to face the problem before it is too late and Pantogar revitalise is the best solution.

Client _
Jacobson Medical (Hong Kong) Ltd.
Agency _
JWT Hong Kong
Creative Directors _
Steven Lee, Barbara Fu, Kwong Chi Kit,
Art Directors _
Arthur Tse
Copywriter _
Daat Lai, Jesse Wong
Region _
Hong Kong

Agency _
Kaffeine Communications
Creative Directors _
Anze Jereb, Dima Tsapko
Art Director _
Denis Pogrebnyak
Copywriter _
Nadia Skrynnyk
Designer _
Roman Davydyu
Illustrator _
Denis Pogrebnyak
Country _
Ukraine

BUILD YOUR YEAR OF GOOD DEEDS

This calendar represents a constructor set made of 16 separate cards with slots which can be joined in any combination. Each card contains a monthly schedule and advice about how to do some good. Additional 4 elements are the agency's business cards. 16 is the quantity that allows construction of a certain figure, e. g. the Rabbit, 2011's Chinese zodiac animal. The main idea of the calendar lies in the possibility to construct a year of good deeds. The calendar is Kaffeine Communications advertising agency's self promo. It was presented as a New Year gift to clients.

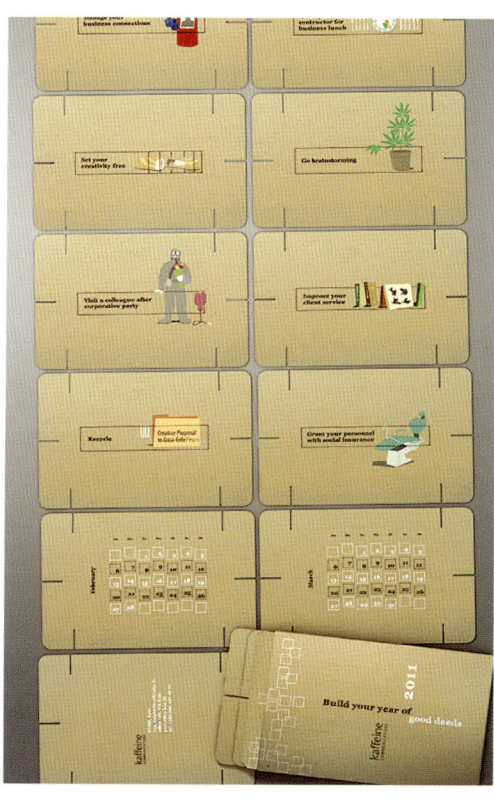

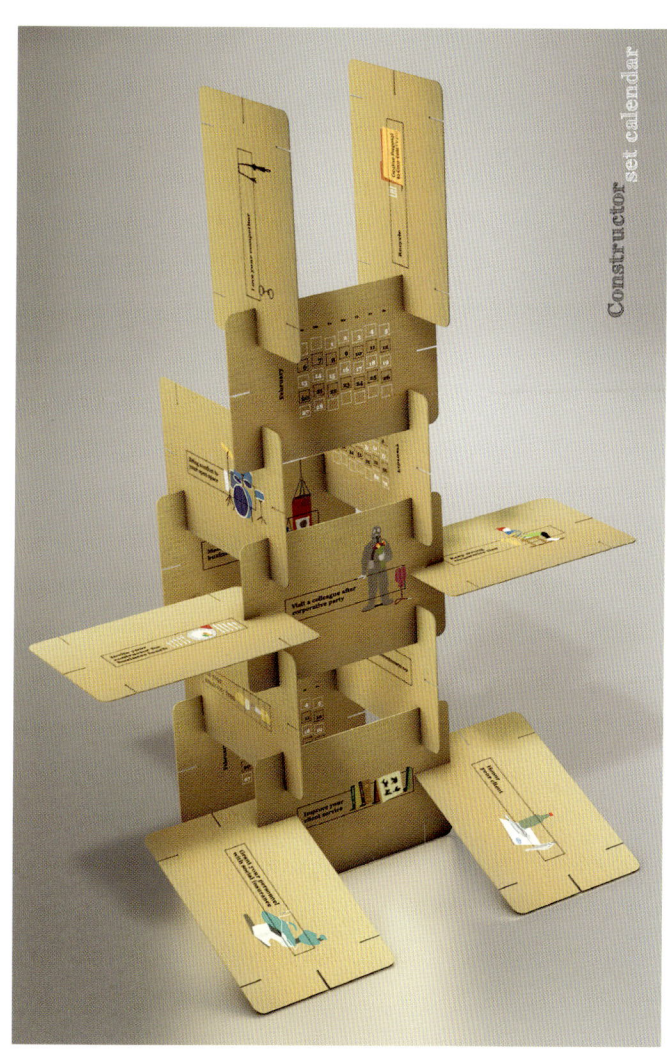

Studio _
Hand Design Studio
Creative Director _
Vinko Pasalic
Designer _
Vinko Pasalic
Photographer _
Igor Sitar
Country _
Croatia

LET'S PLAY WITH FOOD

For 8 years now, our studio has been surprising its clients with Christmas gifts dubbed "Let's Play With Food". Year after year we try to be original and creative, giving away the best of Croatian hand-made food. Some food we actually make ourselves and that is the case with this gift — we baked cookies. Cookies were accompanied with traditional Croatian continental red and white wine together with Biska, an alcoholic drink made out of mistletoe. The headquarters of homemade Biska is in Istria (one of the Croatian peninsulas), in a town called Vrh whose inhabitants supposedly have their own secret recipe and quite often they mix it with a careful ratio of mistletoe and three other types of herbs.

The package/gift represents our hedonistic obsession, an obsession that is almost an addiction. It shows our true colour as it goes hand in hand with our professional endeavours. It was designed to produce vigour, inspire fortune and release tension.

Client _
ArjoWiggins
Studio _
Sensus Design Factory Zagreb
Designer _
Nedjeljko Spoljar
Country _
Croatia

ARJOWIGGINS CURIOUS PARTICLES NOTEBOOK

A promotional notebook for ArjoWiggins Curious Particles paper brand. Besides serving as a nice notebook, the inside pages contain illustrations that demonstrate the paper's printing characteristics and exceptional quality.

Studio _
Matter Strategic Design
Creative Director _
Mike Kasperski
Copywriter _
Oanh Kasperski
Designer _
Mike Kasperski
Country _
Canada

MATTER STRATEGIC DESIGN 2011 NOTEBOOK

For our holiday giveaway, we wanted to create something that was both beautiful and functional, something that would be true to who we are and open to who our clients want to be. The notebook focuses on one basic yet critical question—what matters to you?

In this case, that means 11 poignant and often cheeky visitor - generated quotes compiled from www.matter.to and presented on striking yellow paper at the centre of the notebook.

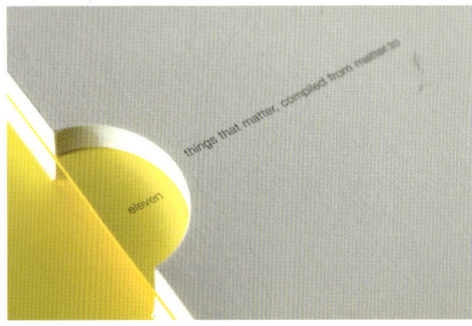

DIFFUSEUR DE BONHEUR

A self-promotion Valentine Card that explores the concept of shared action where the user becomes an actor in the process of creation (and the diffusion of his love). The stencil seemed the medium most fit to perform this idea.
A limited edition cards, silk screened, laser cut and folded by hand to make it feel that every card is special.

Designer _
Oussama Mezher
Country _
Canada

Studio _
Nikolaus Schmidt Design
Designer _
Nikolaus Schmidt
Photographer _
Daniela Beranek
Country _
Austria

SEASON'S GREETINGS 2010/2011

Season's greetings for clients and friends. The maze illustration reflects the year itself.

TWOTHOUSAND11

TWOTHOUSAND11 is a collaboration between OPEN STUDIO and Letterpress 77. Certain colour gradients reflect and illustrate the different seasons of the year. The calendar was sent out to selected clients, partners and friends as a new year gift. It's strictly limited to an edition of 100 — every single one handprinted and therefore unique.

Client _
Open Studio, Letterpress 77
Studio _
Open Studio
Creative Directors _
Kai Hoffmann, Julia Furtmann
Designers _
Julia Furtmann, Kai Hoffmann
Printer _
Kiyo Matsumoto / Letterpress 77
Country _
Germany

PROMOTION GIFT AND GOODS

Studio _
Program Studio
Designer _
Chris May
Country _
Austria

YESTERDAY WAS A BORE

Self promotional mailer for Program Studio, consisting of a poster, 6 stickers and a gray board for backing. The overall concept is a subtle reminder to better appreciate the seemingly mundane everyday experiences we all have. The poster features a series of 100 fill-in-the-blank phrases all written in the first-person voice. The stickers each contain a different phrase chosen from the poster. These have been placed outdoors encouraging anyone to participate. Chosen comments left on these outdoor stickers have been posted to the Program Studio web site.

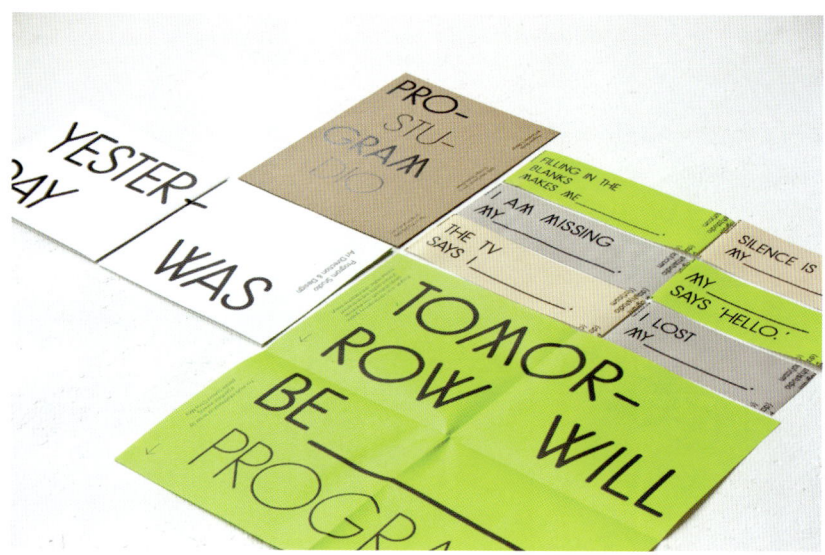

SAYHELLO ON YOUR DESK

This is a "Green" launch event. The concept and creativity of the event came from sayhello, a design studio based in Milan. The eco-friendly gifts were given to all the guests. It was a marketing activity to promote the studio involving all its followers on social networks.

Studio _
sayhello
Creative Directors _
Cecilia Melli, Giulio Urgo
Art Directors _
Cecilia Melli, Giulio Urgo
Copywriter _
Cecilia Melli
Photographer _
Cecilia Melli
Country _
Italy

Client _
Aktion Mensch
Studio _
Strichpunkt Design
Illustrator _
Frauke Berg
Photographer _
Eva Haberle
Country _
Germany

AKTION MENSCH ANNUAL REPORT 2011

Conception, design, composition and production of the annual report for non-profit organization Aktion Mensch.
For the second time in a row, the annual report for the largest lottery in Germany had to combine transparent reporting with exceptional image communication. It should also demonstrate what effects lie behind the funding amounts identified.
Finally, a tear-off calendar was created.
365 days and 365 stories lead the observer through the year and document activities at Aktion Mensch. It's a decorative showpiece that combines a large amount of information with high attention value. The calendar will be complemented by an included magazine, a compact book of figures and media that is accessible for people with disabilities.

DAS WIR GEWINNT

365
TAGE
BILANZ
FINANZBERICHT 2010

www.aktion-mensch.de

AKTION MENSCH
DAS WIR GEWINNT

365
TAGE
GESCHICHTEN
EINBLICKE 2010

www.aktion-mensch.de

13/366 365 TAGE GESCHICHTEN | EINBLICKE 2010

MITTWOCH
13.07.2011
Wednesday | Mercredi | Miércoles | Mercoledì | Onsdag

Sport für alle

14/366 365 TAGE GESCHICHTEN | EINBLICKE 2010

DONNERSTAG
14.07.2011
Thursday | Jeudi | Jueves | Giovedì | Torsdag

über

700

Projekte im Monat

14/366 365 TAGE GESCHICHTEN | EINBLICKE 2010

Die Aktion Mensch unterstützte 2010 monatlich rund 700 Projekte der Behindertenhilfe sowie der Kinder- und Jugendhilfe. Das waren ungefähr 23 am Tag bei genau 8.511 Projekten im gesamten Jahr.

AKTION MENSCH

17/366 365 TAGE GESCHICHTEN | EINBLICKE 2010

SONNTAG
17.07.2011
Sunday | Dimanche | Domingo | Domenica | Söndag

„ NOCH IMMER MÜSSEN
BARRIEREN
IN DEN KÖPFEN
BESEITIGT WERDEN ... „

RENATE REYMANN, PRÄSIDENTIN DES DEUTSCHEN
BLINDEN- UND SEHBEHINDERTENVERBANDES

72/366 365 TAGE GESCHICHTEN | EINBLICKE 2010

SAMSTAG
10.09.2011
Saturday | Samedi | Sábado | Sabato | Lördag

„ HAST
DU
GENUG? „

75/366 365 TAGE GESCHICHTEN | EINBLICKE 2010

DIENSTAG
13.09.2011
Tuesday | Mardi | Martes | Martedì | Tisdag

1
Million
454.384

neue Losteilnehmer

23/366 365 TAGE GESCHICHTEN | EINBLICKE 2010

SAMSTAG
23.07.2011
Saturday | Samedi | Sábado | Sabato | Lördag

Zukunftschancen maßgeschneidert

Studio _
The Allotment Brand Design
Brand Strategist _
Paul Middlebrool, Michael Smith
Art Director _
James Backhurst, Michael Smith
Art Director _
Michael Smith
Designer _
Michael Smith
Copywriter _
Scott Perry
Illustrator _
Geoffery Appleton
Country _
UK

JACK AND THE GIANT RECESSION SELF-PROMOTIONAL BOOK 2011

There is a common thread throughout the work of the The Allotment – we believe passionately that storytelling is the 'key' to effective brand communications and future growth for our clients.
We created this self-promotional fairytale book, it's based on the classic Jack and the Beanstalk fable but with a modern twist. It's simply a story about storytelling and how that can have a positive, profound and transformative impact on the success of brands and businesses.

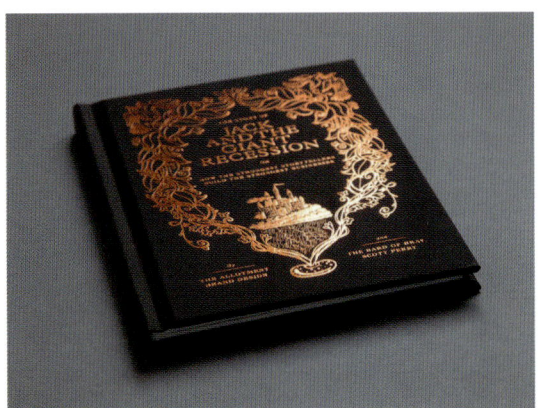

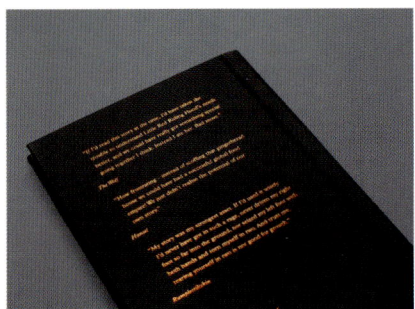
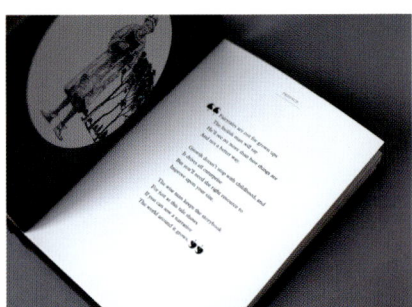
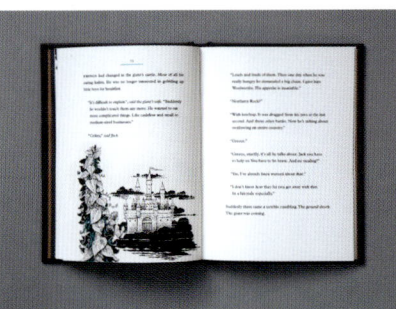

Studio _
The Allotment Brand Design
Creative Directors _
James Backhurst, Michael Smith
Art Director _
Paula Talford
Designer _
James Backhurst, Paula Talford
Copywriter _
James Backhurst, Paula Talford
Typographer _
David Bateman
Country _
UK

WINTER WEDDING INVITATION

A simple typographic twist brings a warm smile to guests invited to a wedding in the depths of winter.
A hand warmer in the shape of a hot water bottle accompanied the invitation.

Studio _
The Allotment Brand Design
Brand Strategies _
Paul Middlebrook, James Backhurst, Paula Talford, Michael Strategy
Art Director _
James Backhurst, Paula Talfor
Designer _
James Backhurst
Copywriter _
Roger Horberry
Illustrator _
Josh Kitney/Photosonic
Country _
Uk

THE ALLOTMENT SELF-PROMOTIONAL MATERIALS

The Allotment London is a branding and design business driven by their passion to help clients grow through storytelling.
Their identity cleverly plays on the iconography associated with allotments. In the United Kingdom allotments are small plots of land given to people in order for them to grow their own food and become self-sufficient and self-sustaining.
Using an up turned 'A' we created a plant pot. Wherever we place this potent symbol growth and transformation happen through the power of great storytelling.

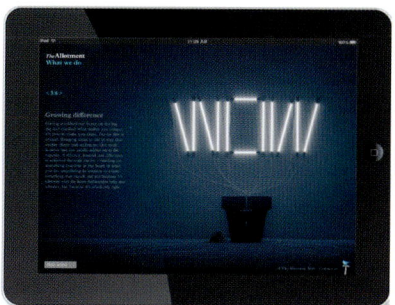

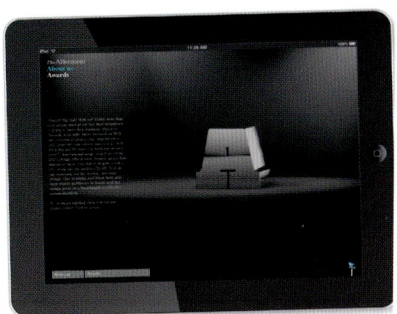

Client _
Copier
Studio _
Zoo Studio
Creative Director _
Gerard Calm
Designer _
Xavier Castells
Photographer _
Ivan Raga
Country _
Spain

COPIER CALENDAR

Promotional calendar for an office equipment company.

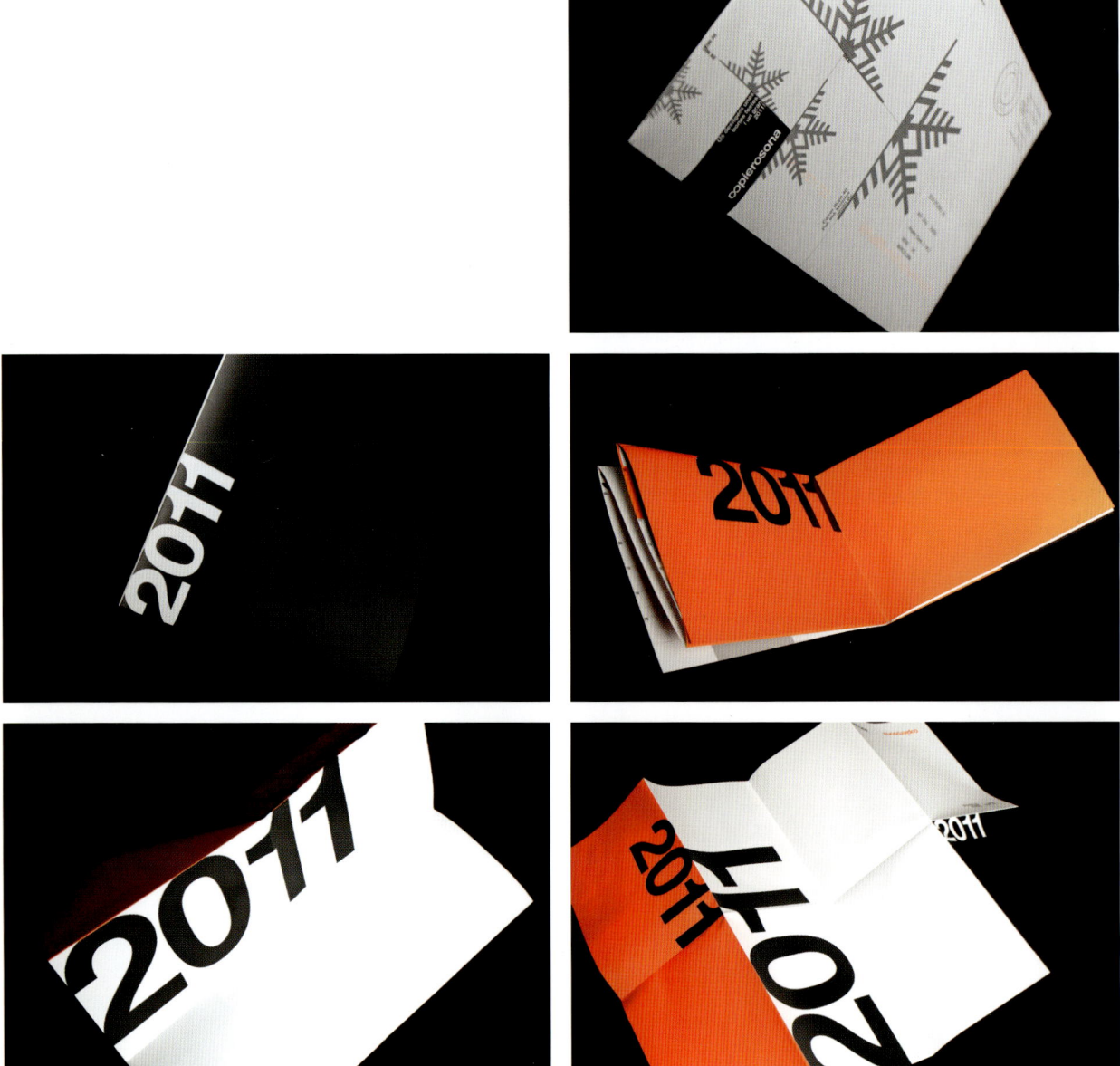

.V. 14
75B 22-23
Alex Egner 24-25
Alpha245 / Leo Burnett 148
Andi Yanto 193
Anti 26-29, 206-207
Beats 152-153
BFG Communications 208
Bigdog Creative 192
Browns 102
Bruketa & Zinic OM 154-155
Bunch 108-109, 156-157
Busybuilding 30-31
BUTTER GmbH 208-209
Campo 110
Chez Valois 175-176
Cole & Weber United 32-39, 212
D+ 142-143
Daniel Gómez 158
DDB Brasil 177
Design Friendship 40-43, 213
Devon Drumm 194-195
Drehmoment Agentur für kreatives Marketing 159
EDENSPIEKERMANN AMSTERDAM 90-91
ENFANTS TERRIBLES / EBOLAINDUSTRIES 178
Eps51 Graphic Design Studio 16-17
Estudio Ibán Ramón 111
F33 179, 209
Gardens & Co. 44
G Design Studio 112-113
GHG Australia 98-99
GJP ADVERTISING + DESIGN Toronto 215

INDEX

GR/DD 196
Grey Milan 160
H-57 srl 197
Hand Design Studio 216-217, 220
Hatch Design 134-135
Havas City 18-19
Hom+Gang 52-53
Hort 103-105, 150-151
Ilovedust 106-107
Interabang 198-199
Jacob Baas 212
Jessica Walsh 46-49, 54-57
Julia Kim 200
JWT 58-59, 132-133, 218
Kaffeine Communications 219
Leo Burnett 60, 214
Lundgren+Lindqvist 70, 180-181
Magpie Studio 74-75
Martha Robertson, Alfonso Sotelo Nava 201
Mash 118
Matter Strategic Design 222
m Barcelona 72-73
Memac Ogilvy 15, 162-163, 188-189
Motherbird 76
Murmure Agency 182-183
Musa Work Lab 120-124
Nikolaus Schmidt Design 224
Open Studio 225
Oussama Mezher 223
Pitertsev Mikhail 119, 126-129, 136-137
POGO 20-21, 78-79
Program Studio 130, 226

Publicis Agency Paris 71
RAPP 164
Raúl Cepi 149, 165
Rethink Communications 184-185, 202-201
RDB CG 80-83
Rudi de Wet Studio 77
Saatchi & Saatchi 161,174
Sayhello 227
Scholz & Friends Berlin 84-87
Sensus Design Factory Zagreb 221
SILO 88-89
Six Inches Communication Pvt. Ltd. 45, 166-167
Sophia Georgopoulou 186
Strange Design 187
Strichpunkt Design 228-229
Studio Brave 131
Takt Studio 168-169
TBWA 61-69, 94-95
The Allotment Brand Design 230-233
The Chase 170-171
Tomato Košir s. p. 138-139
Underline Studio 125
Wildfire Idea 140-141
Wonksite Studio 114-117
Zig 92-93
Zoo Studio 96-97, 144-145, 234-235

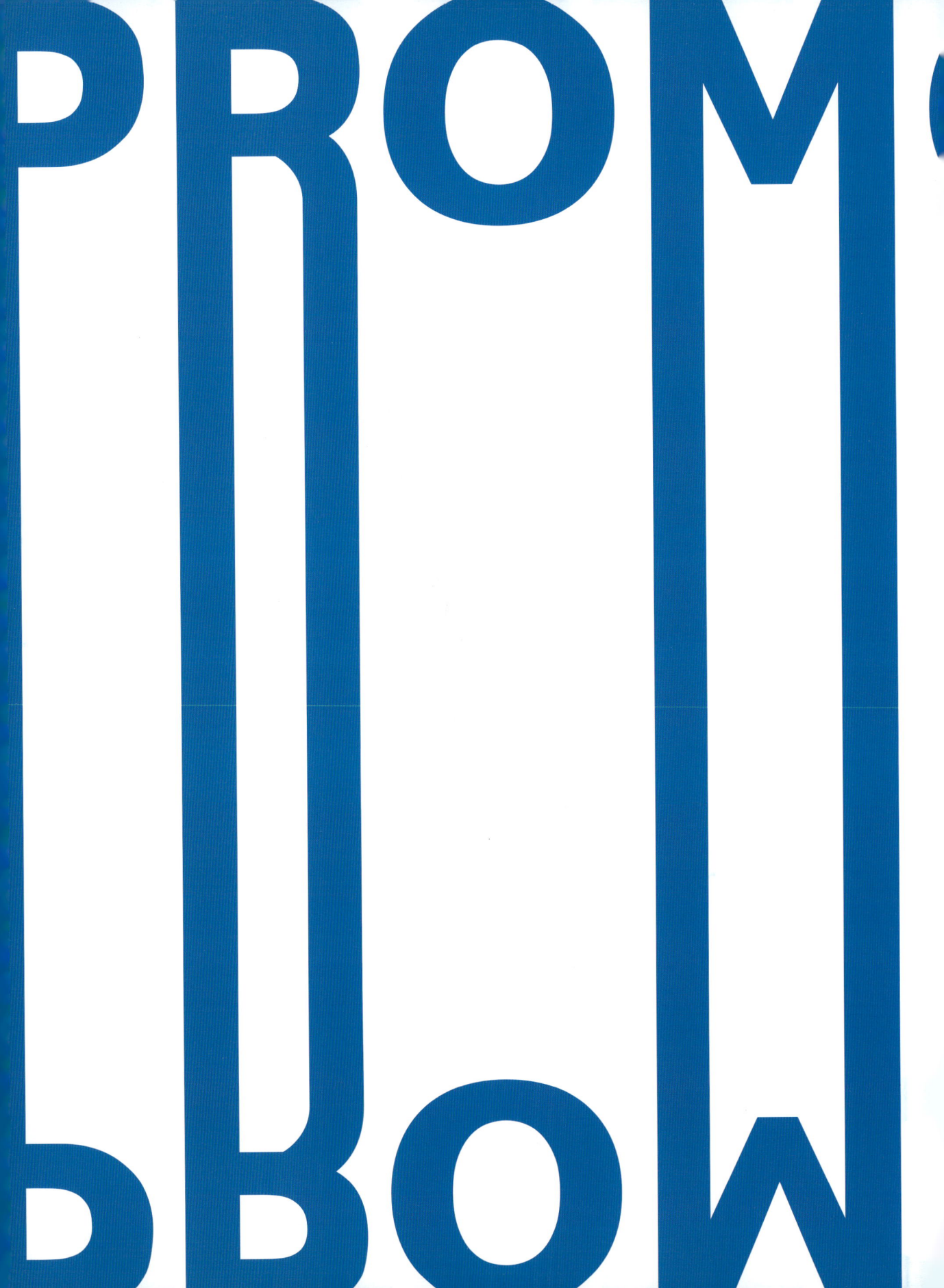

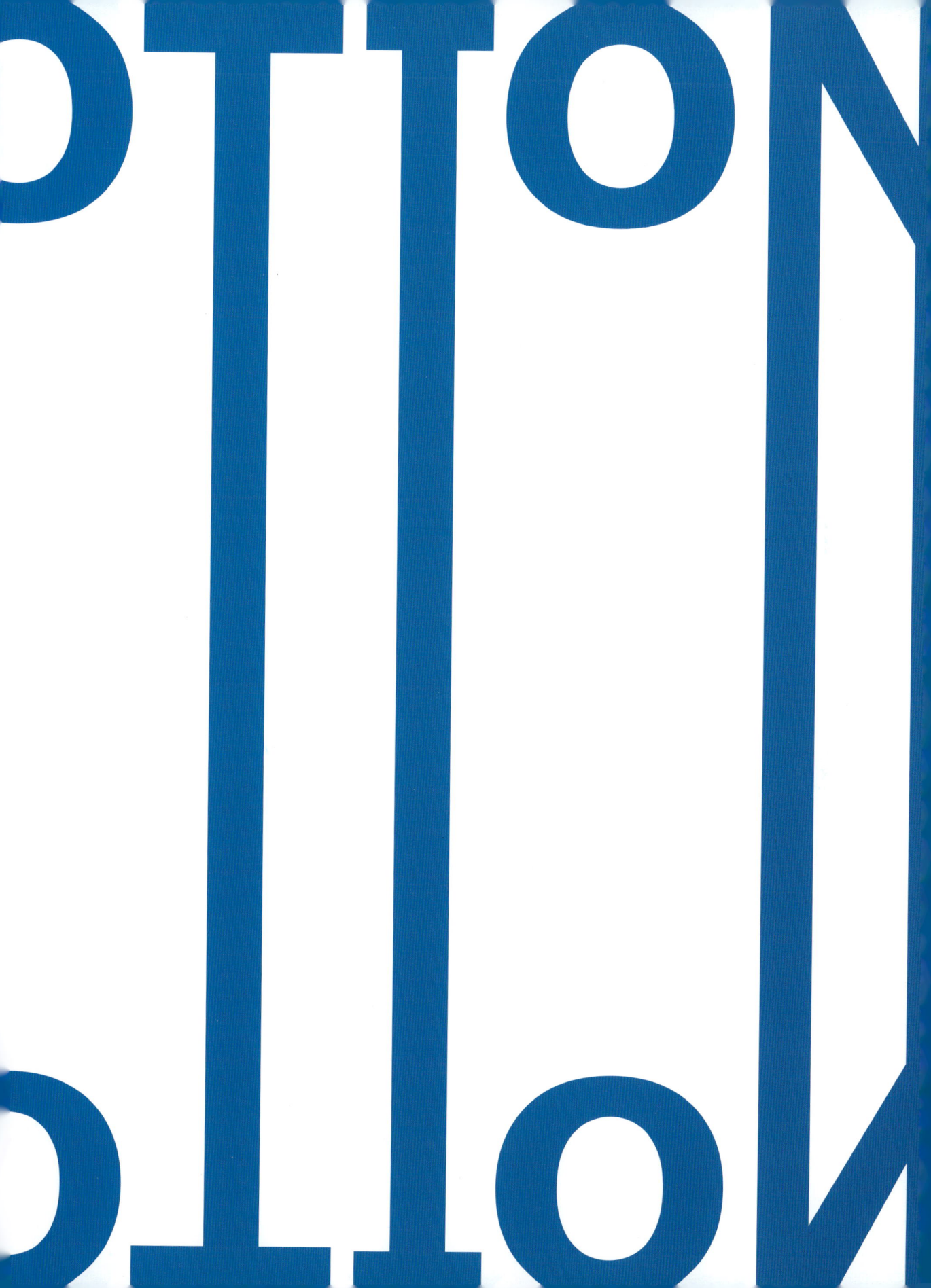